The Cognitive Abili

Practice Tests and Training Guides for The Cognitive Abilities Test CogAT® Grade 4 (Level 11)

by Polemics Applications

Polemics Applications

Polemics Applications LLC produces educational books and apps for the iPhone, iPad and Android platforms. If you enjoy the content of this book feel free to look us up on the App Store and Google Play. Our website is www.polemicsapps.com.

If you find a mistake we would love to fix it.
If you have comments we would love to hear them.
Please send email to **polemicsapp@yahoo.com**

Introduction

The struggle is what matters; this book is not just a practice test to toss at a child. It is a training guide. The language of all of our explanations, tips and tricks have a parental tone. To get maximum effect work through this book's sample tests and then review the answers together. Our appendices in the back not only tell you the answer but how to get to the answer. In all of these areas we are training the student's ability to think critically about each problem.

This book covers the nine categories of questions that your child will see on the grade school CogAT® tests. The material in this book is original in design and modeled after practice tests available online and from feedback from many forum discussions. In certain instances, we have increased the difficulty of the questions beyond the grade level of the student. The important lesson here is for the child to practice struggling with questions. The application of critical thinking in the face of uncertainty is a mainstay of all gifted and talented testing.

To test your child, simply take a sheet of scratch paper and have them mark the answers to each question. The answers to the questions are in the back of the book. As a bonus, for each visual type question we will redisplay the question and explain how you get to the correct answer. Good luck!

Be sure to check out Appendix F for some fun lessons on how to improve critical thinking.

Our objectives for the student:

- ✓ Gain confidence through practice and review of each problem
- ✓ Learn how trick-questions are made and how to beat them
- ✓ Increase critical thinking skills for lifelong use

Table of Contents

Visual Analysis
Figure Classification..7
Figure Matrices..29
Paper Folding...56

Numeric Skills
Number Series...75
Number Puzzles...80
Number Analogies..84

Language Skills
Sentence Completion..106
Verbal Classification...110
Verbal Analogies...116

Appendices
Appendix A: Figure Classification Answer Guide..............122
Appendix B: Figure Matrices Answer Guide....................142
Appendix C: Paper Folding Answer Guide.......................167
Appendix D: Number Series Tips..................................183
Appendix E: Number Puzzles Explained.........................189
Appendix F: Critical Thinking, Testing Tips & Exercises.....193

Each part of this book contains a full-length quiz on the subjects you'll find in the actual COGAT test. We have separated the sections into three broad categories: Visual Analysis, Language Skills and Numeric Skills. Each section has three different areas to test. At the end of each test is an answer key. We recommend you go through the tests writing answers on a piece of paper and then check your work with the answer key.

The appendices in this book are to help train you for certain material on the test. In appendix A-C we actually repeat every question found on the test and tell you how to get to the right answer. In Appendix D and E we will show you the tips and tricks to the number type questions. Appendix F is a set of essays on how to think critically and achieve the best scores on the exam.

Visual Analysis

Visual Analysis

This book is best used as a training guide. When it comes to visual analysis and pattern recognition it is important to make distinctions on different levels. For example, is the pattern presented color based? Shape based? Or number based? Maybe a little of each?

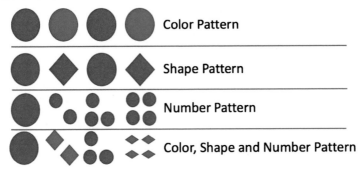

Color Pattern

Shape Pattern

Number Pattern

Color, Shape and Number Pattern

Sometimes Shapes will rotate or turn in a question. This is important clue to the right answer.

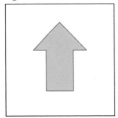 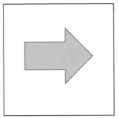 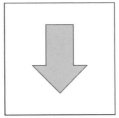 

Sometimes the pictures have a lot of **noise.** This is when there are parts of a picture that are just there to confuse you. In this sample what is consistent in each picture? It's the blue heart. All of those other shapes are there to mislead you. While everything may be a clue to the answer some parts of the picture are really there just as a distraction.

   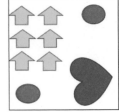

Visual Analysis: Figure Classification

In Figure Classification you are going to be looking at three pictures and you will think about how they are familiar. Maybe each picture has the same colors or shapes or they are arranged in a certain way. Find what is common among all the pictures. Then pick an answer that has the most common features to the three pictures presented. There is often more than one thing in common so be sure to study the pictures in many ways before answering the question.

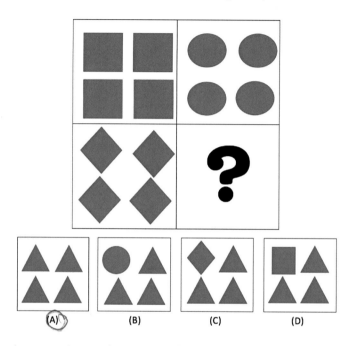

Here is a simple example. In this series of pictures, you see each one has four shapes that are all the same type. The classification is "All shapes in the picture are of the same kind", Answer A shows four triangles. All other answers do not show four of the same shape.

WARNING: These are made HARD its ok to miss these as long as you are practicing looking for common features among the shapes

Figure Classification: Question 1

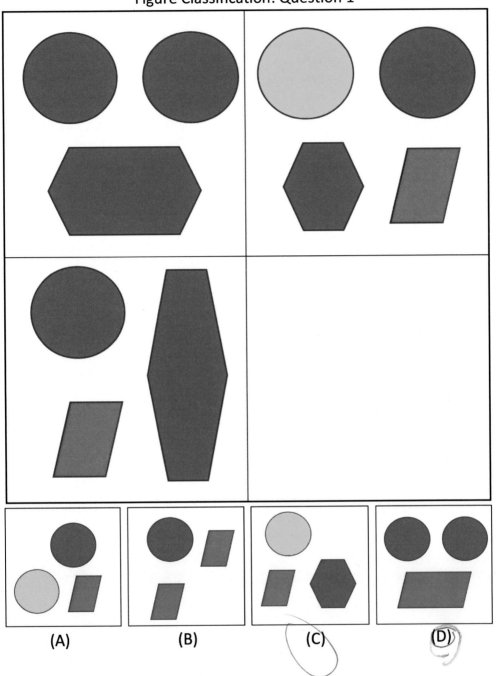

(A)   (B)   (C)   (D)

Figure Classification: Question 2

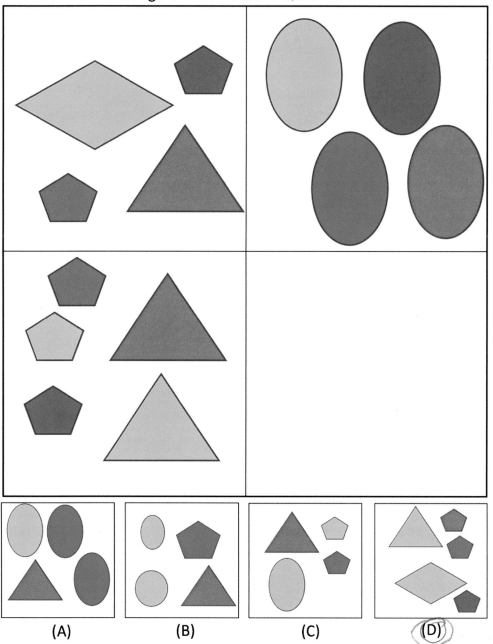

(A)   (B)   (C)   (D)

Figure Classification: Question 3

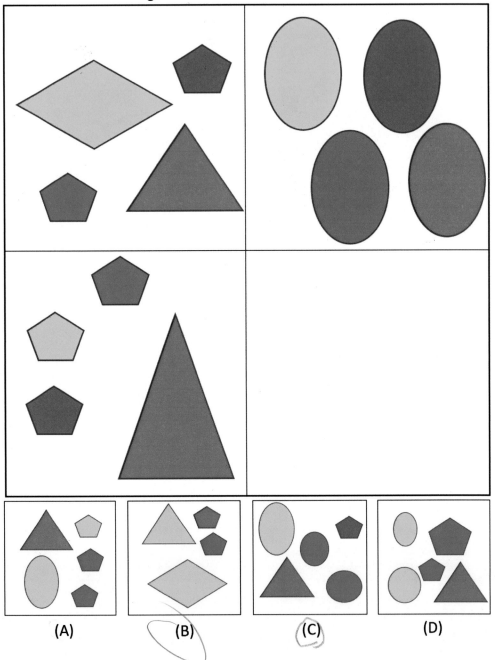

(A) (B) (C) (D)

10

Figure Classification: Question 4

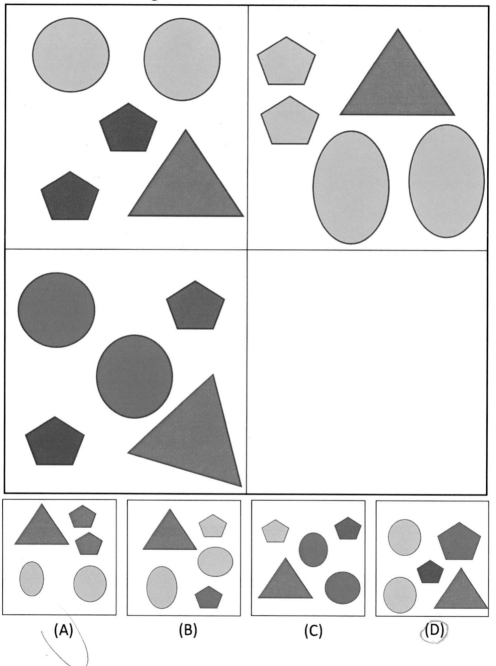

(A)   (B)   (C)   (D)

Figure Classification: Question 5

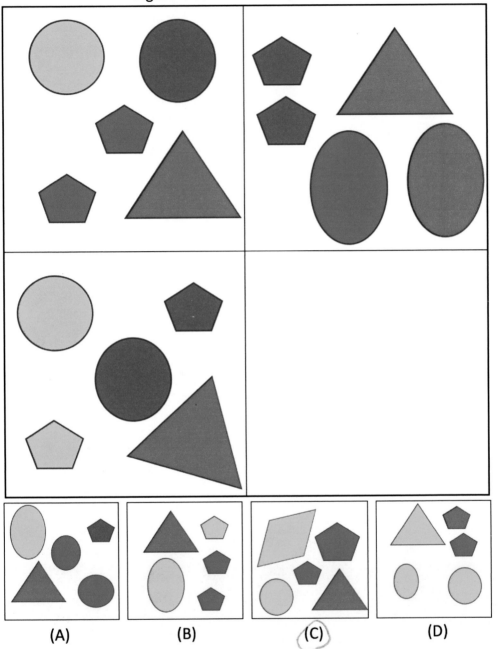

(A)   (B)   (C)   (D)

Figure Classification: Question 6

(A)   (B)   (C)   (D)

Figure Classification: Question 7

(A) (B) (C) (D)

Figure Classification: Question 8

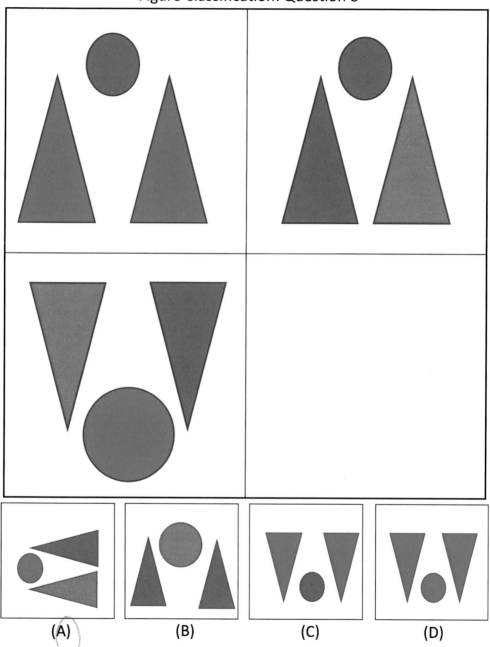

(A) (B) (C) (D)

Figure Classification: Question 9

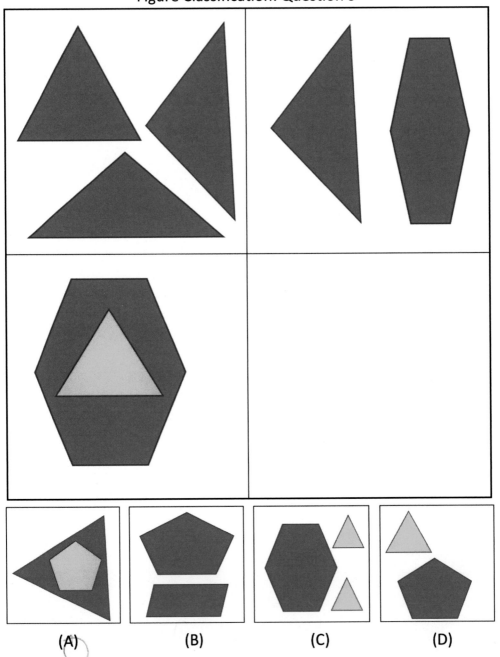

(A)   (B)   (C)   (D)

Figure Classification: Question 10

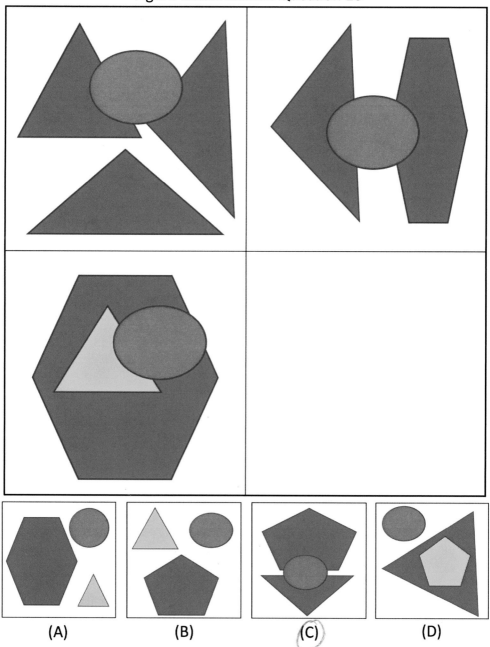

(A)   (B)   (C)   (D)

Figure Classification: Question 11

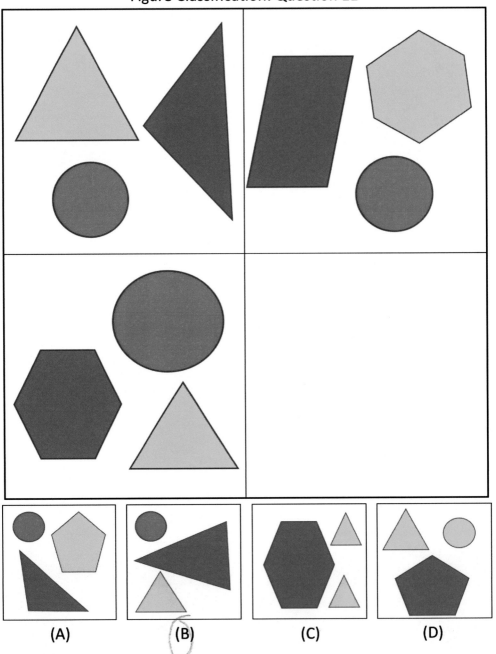

(A)　　　　　(B)　　　　　(C)　　　　　(D)

Figure Classification: Question 12

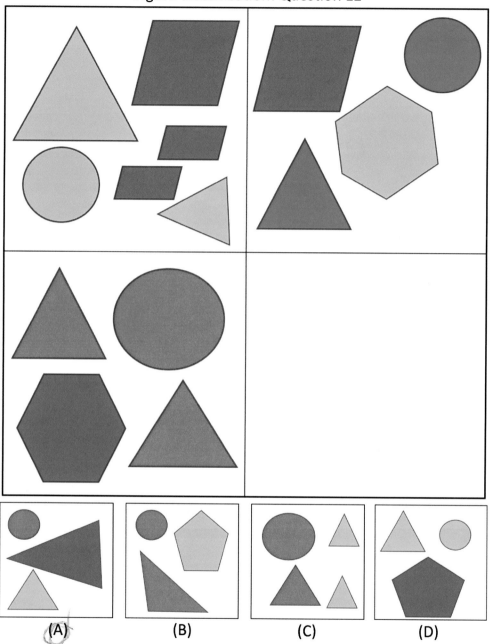

(A)   (B)   (C)   (D)

19

Figure Classification: Question 13

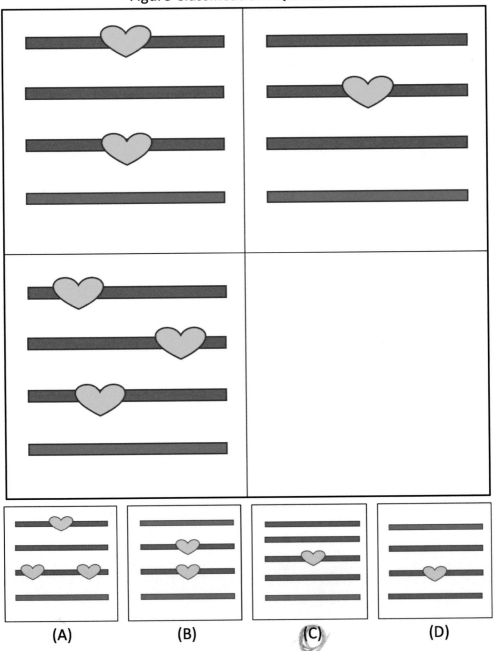

(A)   (B)   (C)   (D)

Figure Classification: Question 14

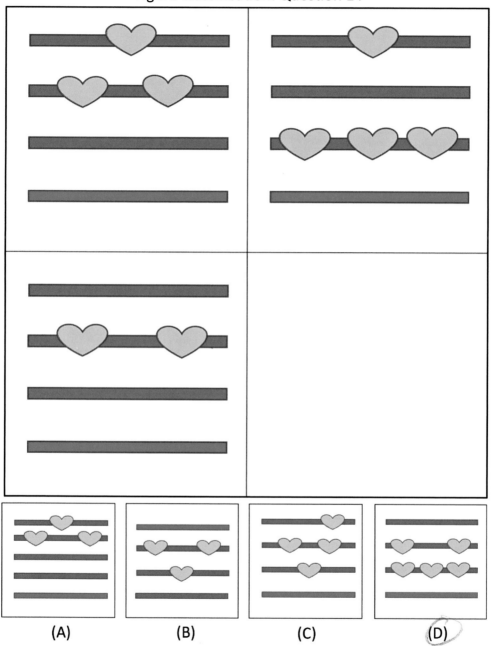

(A)   (B)   (C)   (D)

Figure Classification: Question 15

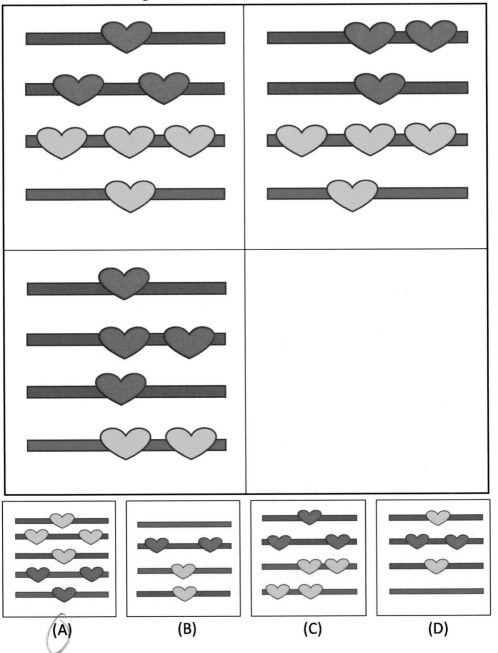

(A)　　　　　(B)　　　　　(C)　　　　　(D)

22

Figure Classification: Question 16

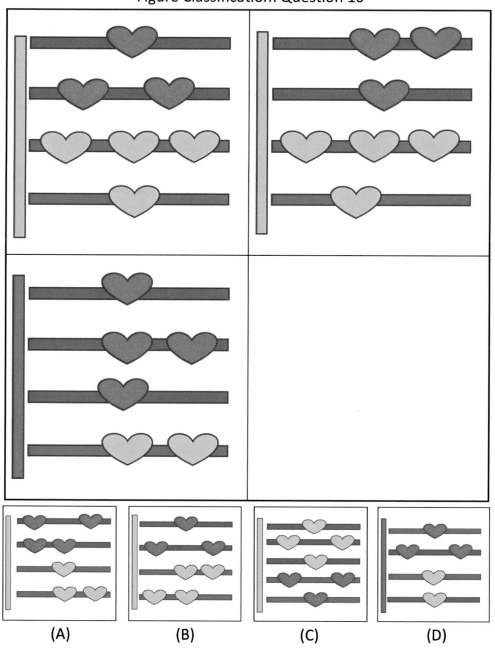

(A) (B) (C) (D)

Figure Classification: Question 17

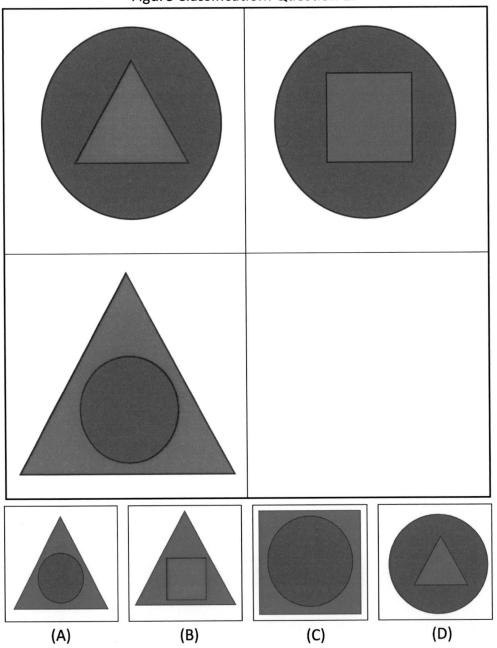

(A)   (B)   (C)   (D)

Figure Classification: Question 18

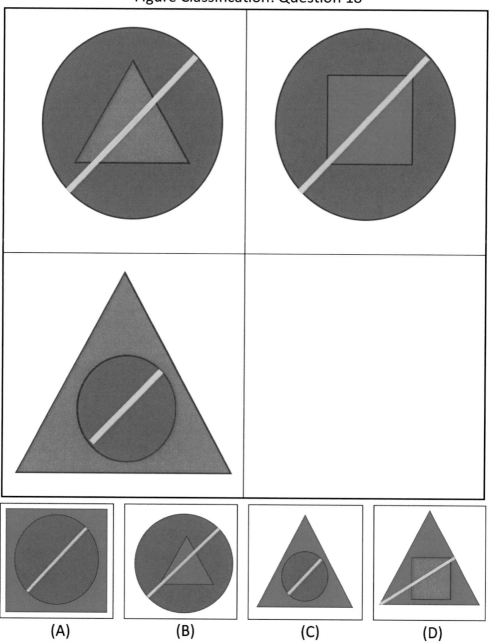

(A)   (B)   (C)   (D)

Figure Classification: Question 19

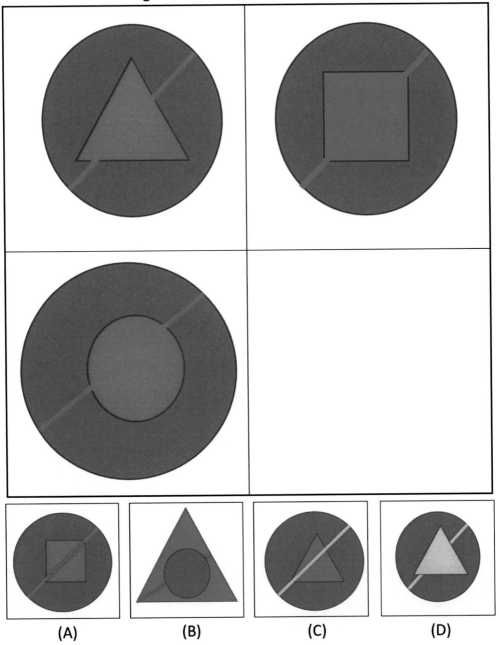

(A)　　　　(B)　　　　(C)　　　　(D)

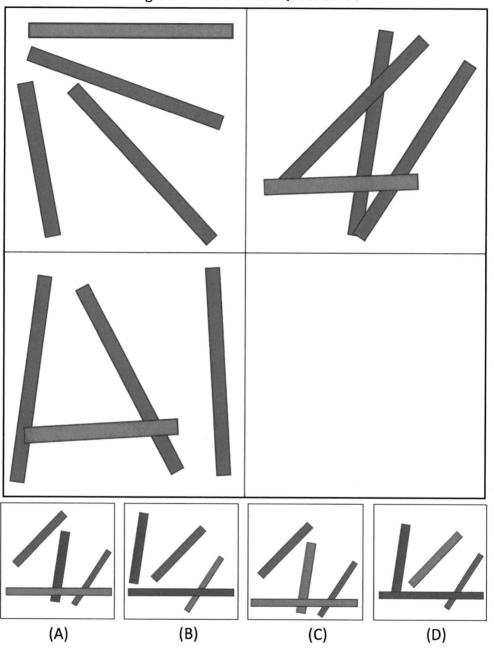

(A) (B) (C) (D)

Figure Classification: Answer Key

Question	Answer
1	C
2	D
3	B
4	A
5	D
6	C
7	A
8	C
9	B
10	C
11	A
12	B or D
13	A
14	D
15	C
16	B
17	C
18	A
19	D
20	A

Please See Appendix A for a detailed explanation for each of these answers. Appendix A is written for adults to explain to the student how a piece of critical thinking occurred on a problem. Tip: use this review time as a discussion platform on other ways the child may have found the answers.

Visual Analysis: Figure Matrices

The figures in each pattern follow a pattern. The pattern reads from left to right and top to bottom. Pick the next picture to complete the pattern. Ask yourself these questions:

- Do the shapes change size?
- Do the number of shapes go up or down?
- Do the colors of the shapes change?
- Are the shapes on top of each other or separated?
- Did the shapes rotate?
- How many sides does each shape have in the pattern?

Any one or more of these questions can assist you in finding the pattern.

In the below example the top left white box rotates to the left AND changes colors to orange. When looking at this problem we can ask "what happened to the white box?" Then we can say "The white box rotated and changed colors to orange" Next we can look at the blue triangle and ask, "What will the blue triangle look like when it rotates and changes color to orange?" The answer is (D). Now practice this thought process on the questions in this section.

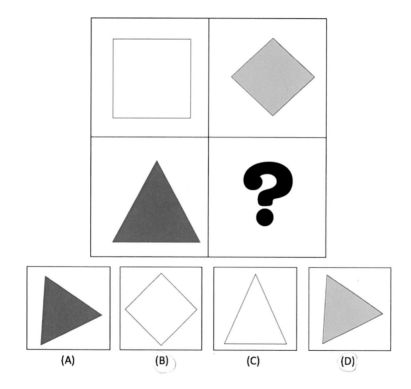

Figure Matrices: Question 1

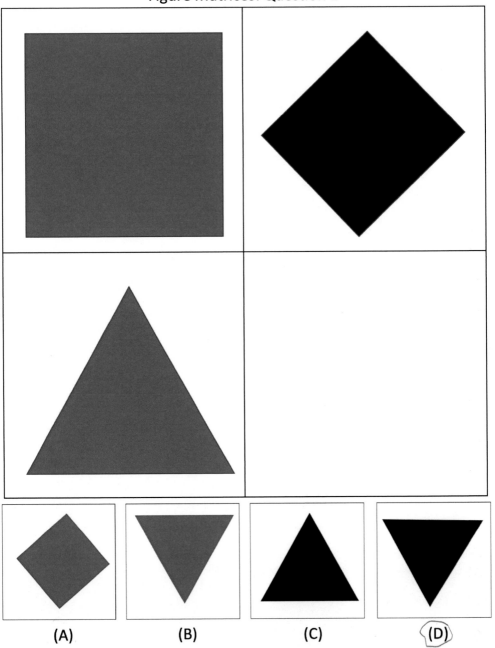

(A)　　　　(B)　　　　(C)　　　　(D)

Figure Matrices: Question 2

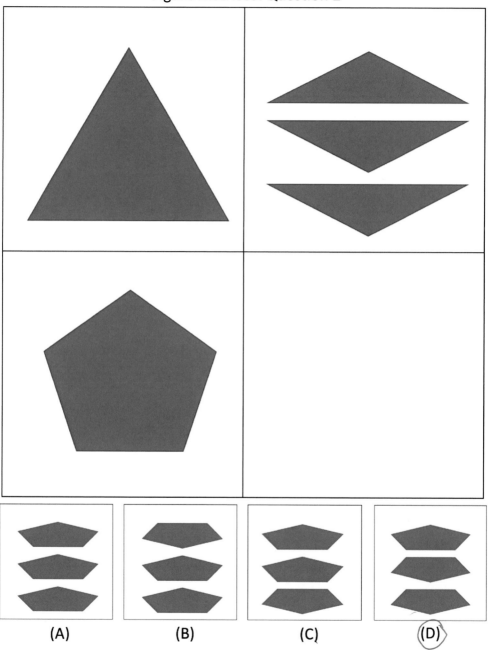

(A)   (B)   (C)   (D)

Figure Matrices: Question 3

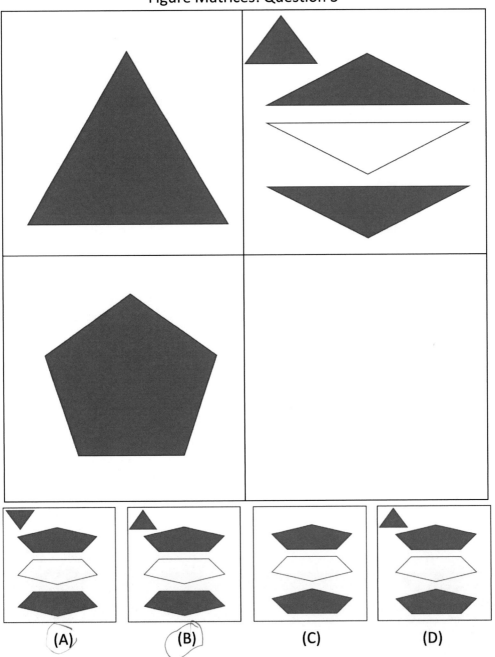

(A) (B) (C) (D)

Figure Matrices: Question 4

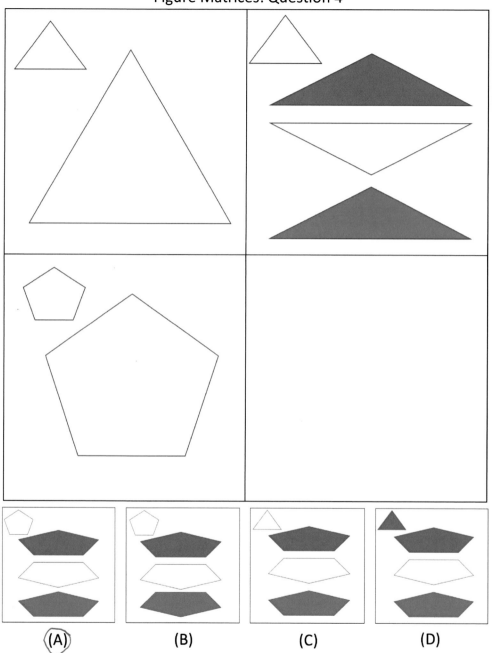

(A) (B) (C) (D)

Figure Matrices: Question 5

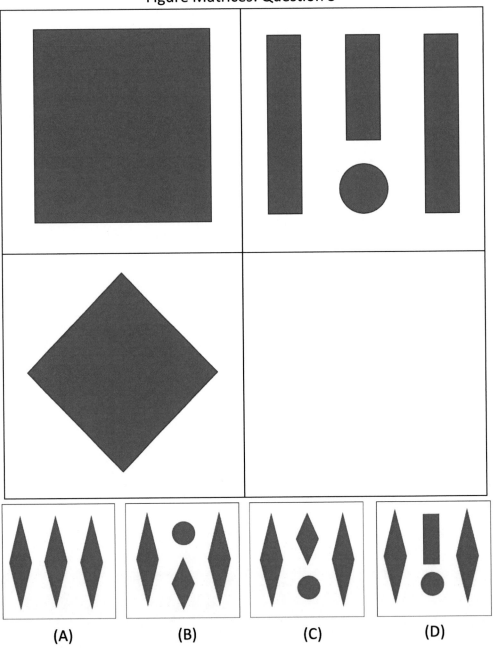

(A)   (B)   (C)   (D)

Figure Matrices: Question 6

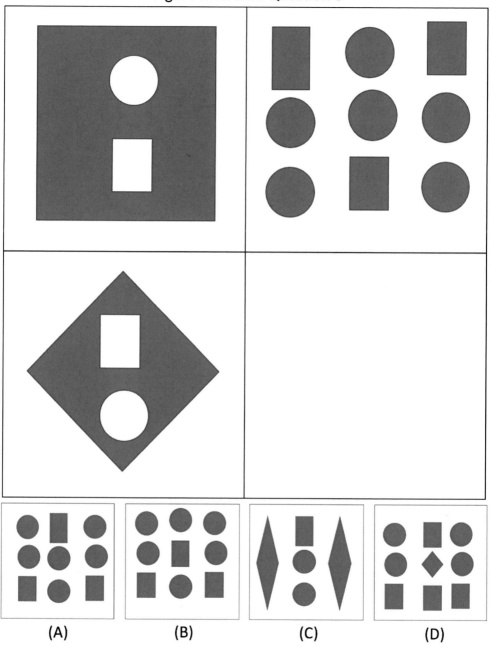

(A)   (B)   (C)   (D)

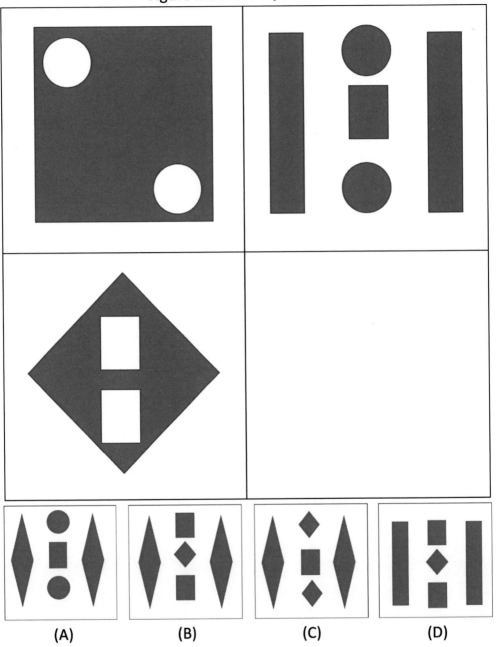

Figure Matrices: Question 8

(A)   (B)   (C)   (D)

Figure Matrices: Question 9

(A)   (B)   (C)   (D)

Figure Matrices: Question 10

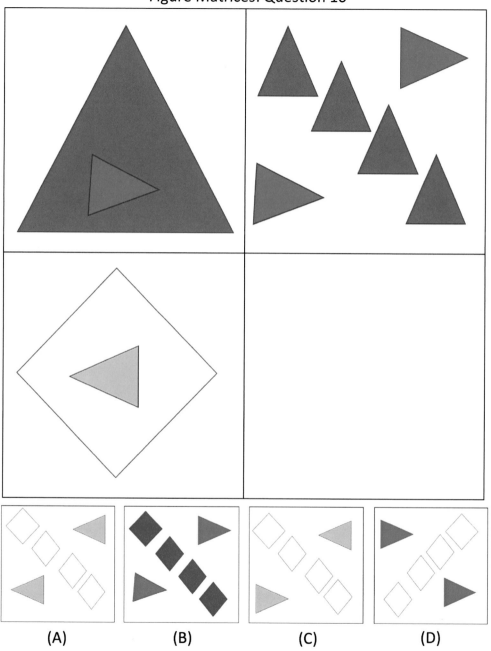

(A)   (B)   (C)   (D)

Figure Matrices: Question 11

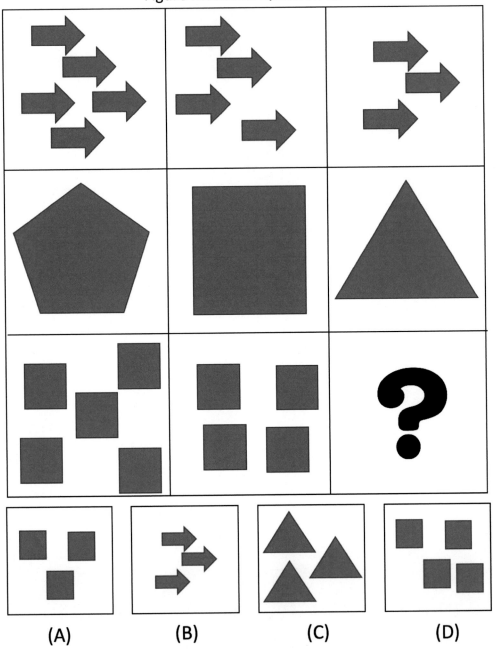

(A)   (B)   (C)   (D)

Figure Matrices: Question 12

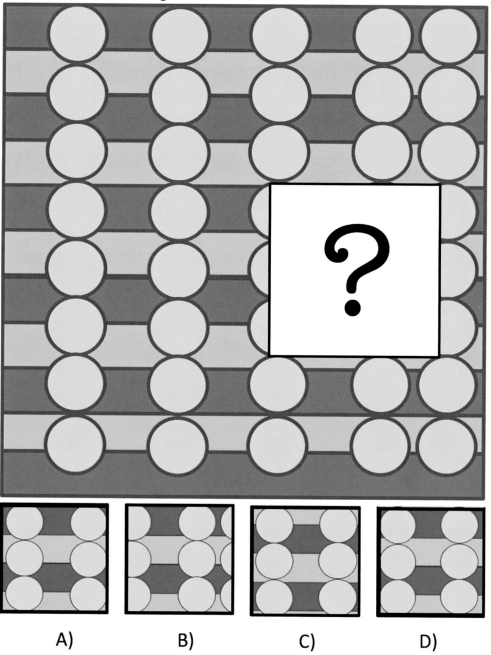

A)   B)   C)   D)

A)   B)   C)   D)

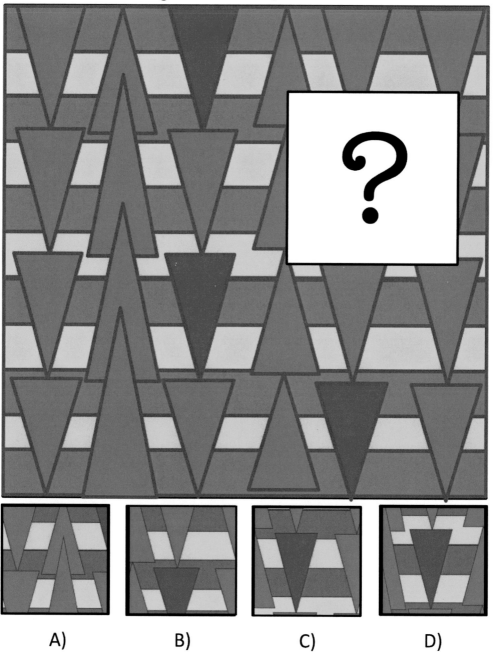

A)   B)   C)   D)

Figure Matrices: Question 15

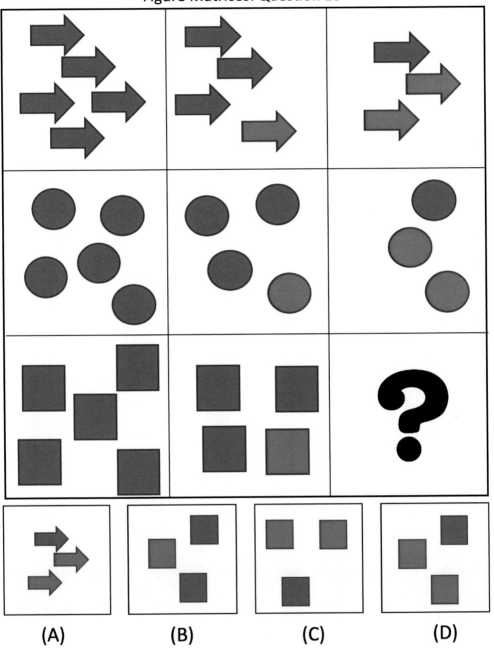

(A)   (B)   (C)   (D)

A)   B)   C)   D)

Figure Matrices: Question 17

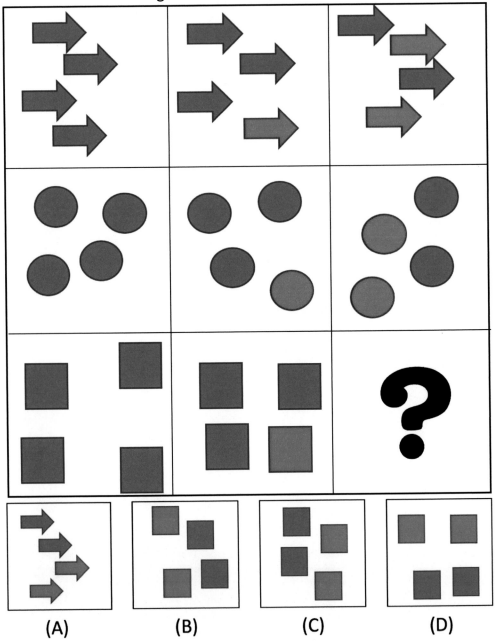

(A)   (B)   (C)   (D)

Figure Matrices: Question 18

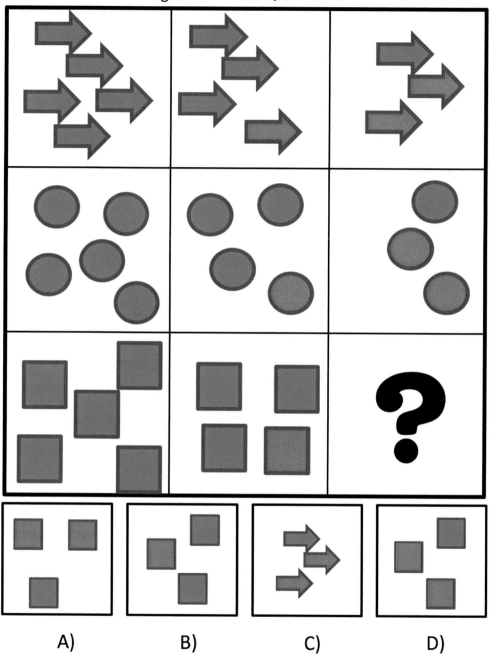

A)   B)   C)   D)

Figure Matrices: Question 19

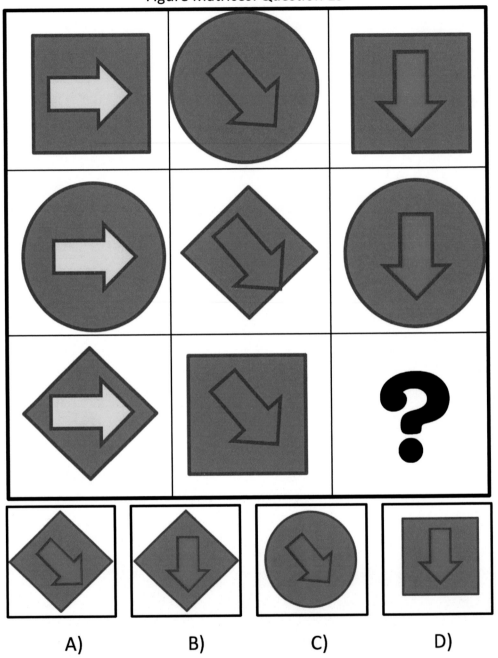

A)   B)   C)   D)

Figure Matrices: Question 20

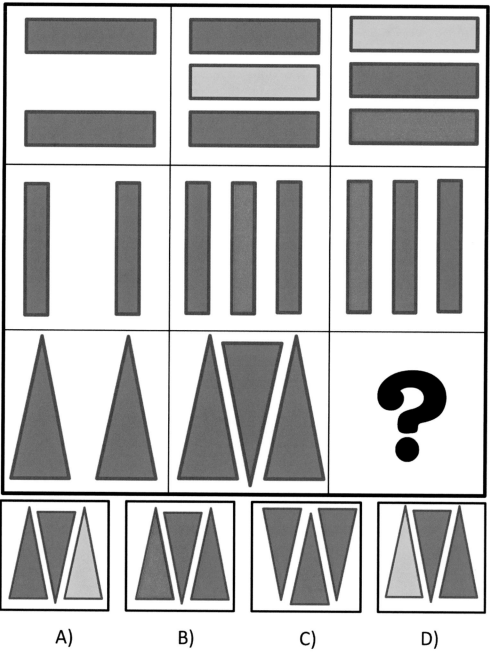

A)

B)

C)

D)

Figure Matrices: Question 21 (Bonus)

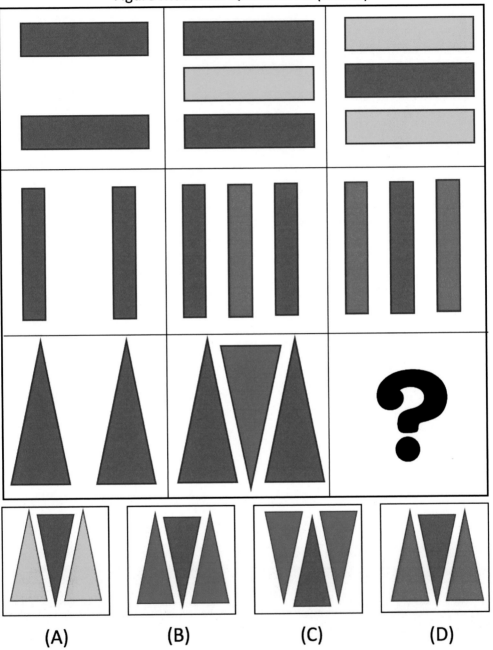

(A) (B) (C) (D)

Figure Matrices: Question 22 (Bonus)

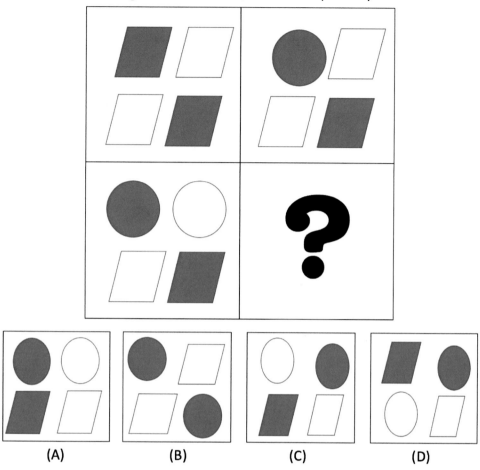

(A)   (B)   (C)   (D)

Figure Matrices: Question 23 (Bonus)

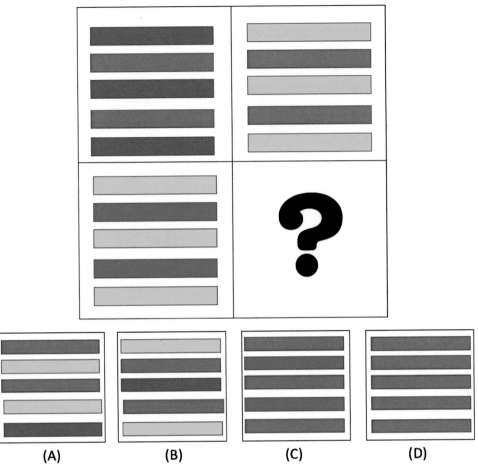

(A)   (B)   (C)   (D)

Figure Matrices: Question 24 (Bonus)

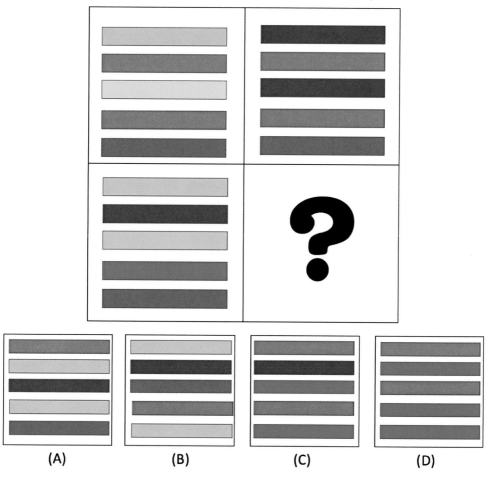

(A) (B) (C) (D)

Figure Matrices: Question 25 (Bonus)

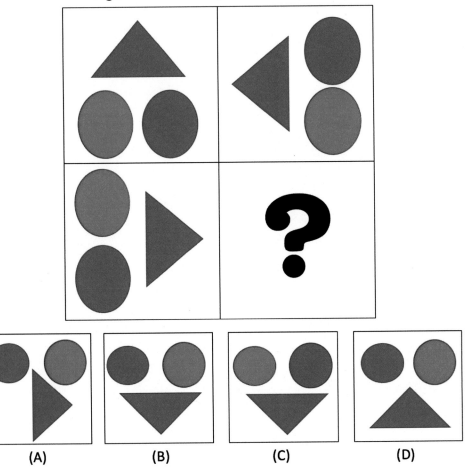

(A)   (B)   (C)   (D)

Figure Matrices: Answer Key

Question	Answer
1	D
2	D
3	B
4	A
5	C
6	A
7	B
8	D
9	C
10	A
11	A
12	B
13	D

Question	Answer
14	C
15	D
16	C
17	B
18	D
19	B
20	B
21	B
22	B
23	C
24	A
25	B

Please See Appendix B for a detailed explanation for each of these answers. Appendix B is written for adults to explain to children how a piece of critical thinking occurred on a problem. Tip: use this review time as a discussion platform on other ways the child may have found the answers. Note: Questions 20-25 were from a different (but similar) Gifted and Talented Test Trainer, congrats if you answered all of them correctly!

Visual Analysis: Paper Folding

Paper folding is a practice of visualizing symmetry. Each question shows a piece of paper that is folded and cut. The answers all show what the paper will look like when it was unfolded. You can make a quick demonstration of this by folding a piece of paper in half and cutting a half heart shape out and then showing how it looks when unfolded.

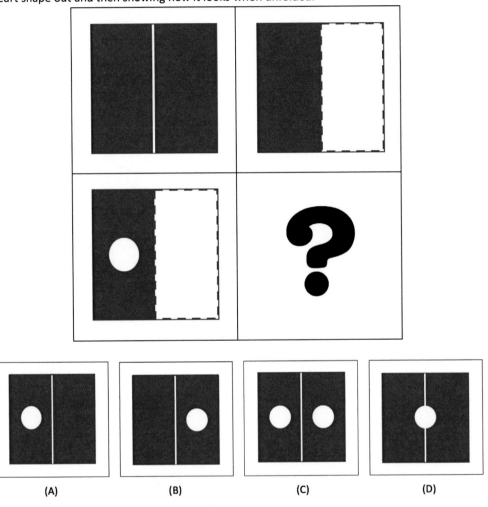

(A)   (B)   (C)   (D)

Let's do the first one together. Here the paper is folded in half along the white line, then a hole is punched. Which answer shows what the paper looks like unfolded? Answer C is correct; it shows two holes punched in the proper (symmetrical) locations.

Paper Folding: Question 1

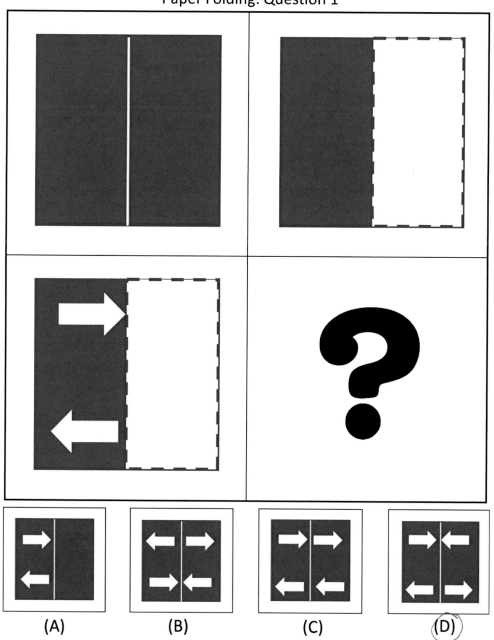

(A)   (B)   (C)   (D)

Paper Folding: Question 2

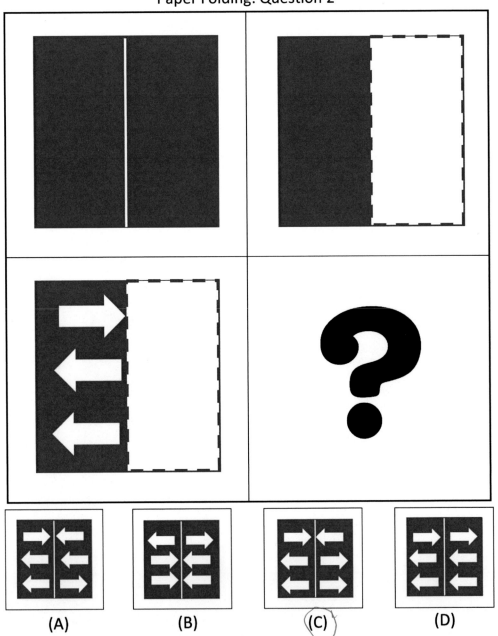

(A) (B) (C) (D)

Paper Folding: Question 3

(A)　　　(B)　　　(C)　　　(D)

Paper Folding: Question 4

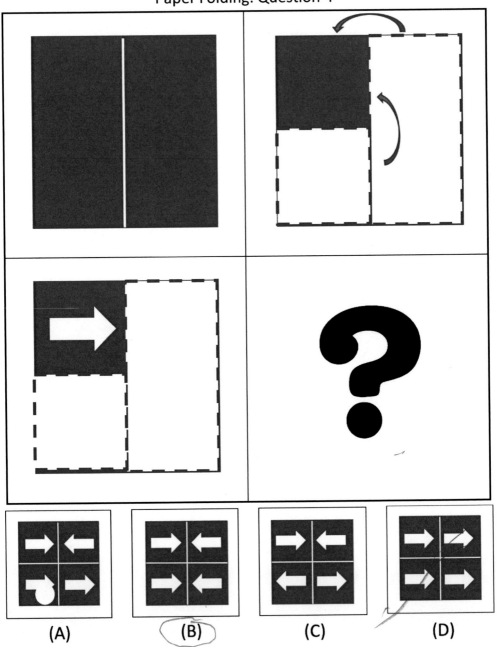

(A) (B) (C) (D)

Paper Folding: Question 5

(A)   (B)   (C)   (D)

Paper Folding: Question 6

(A)   (B)   (C)   (D)

Paper Folding: Question 7

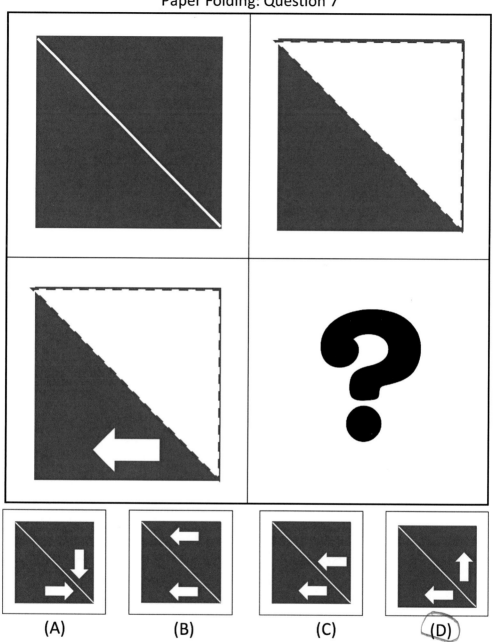

(A)　　　　(B)　　　　(C)　　　　(D)

Paper Folding: Question 8

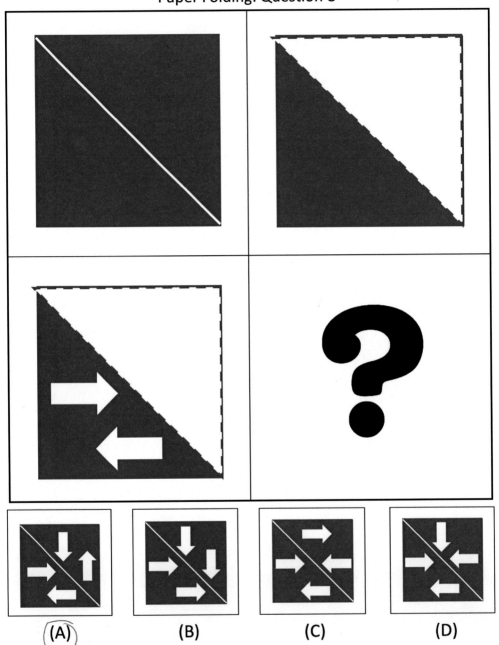

Paper Folding: Question 9

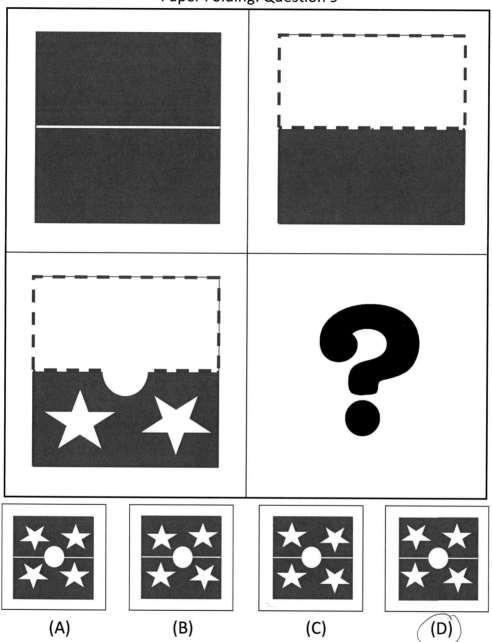

(A) (B) (C) (D)

Paper Folding: Question 10

(A)   (B)   (C)   (D)

Paper Folding: Question 11

(A)　　　　　(B)　　　　　(C)　　　　　(D)

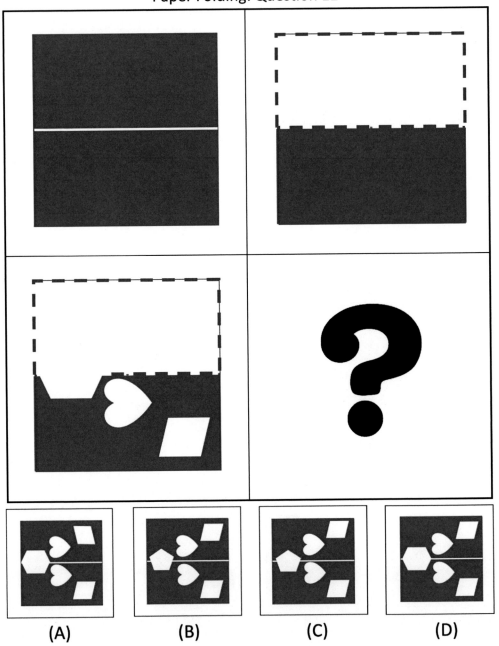

(A)　　　　(B)　　　　(C)　　　　(D)

(A)   (B)   (C)   (D)

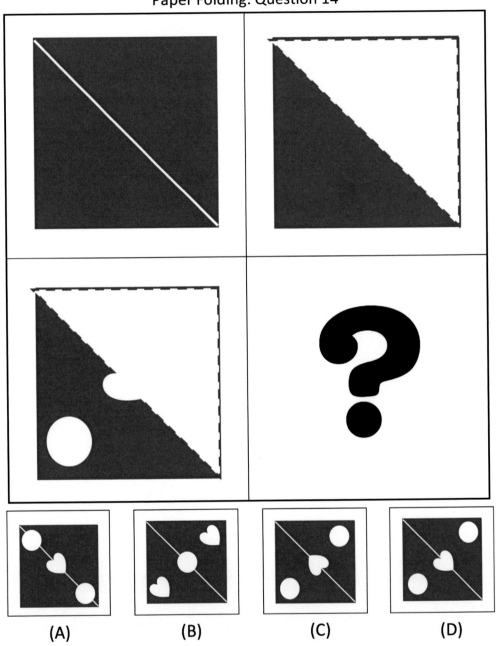

(A)   (B)   (C)   (D)

Paper Folding: Question 15

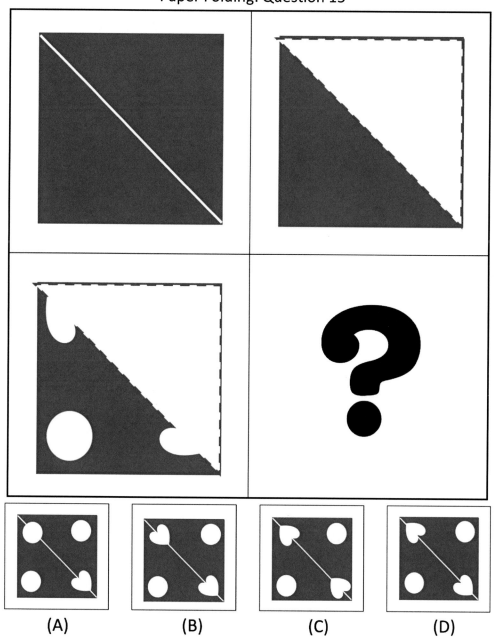

(A)   (B)   (C)   (D)

Paper Folding: Question 16

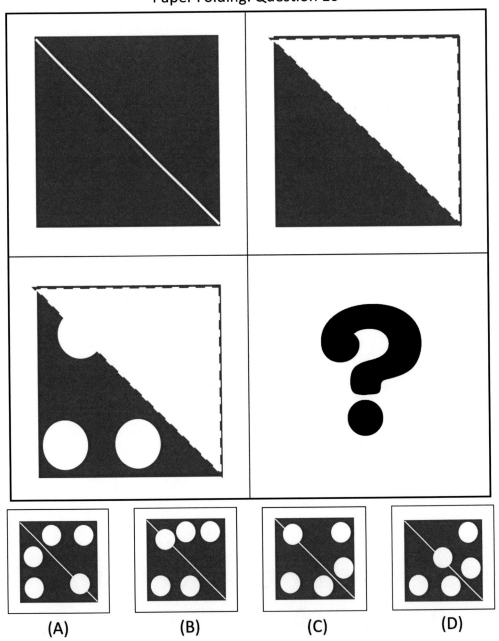

(A)   (B)   (C)   (D)

Paper Folding: Answer Key

Question	Answer
1	D
2	C
3	D
4	B
5	D
6	B
7	D
8	A
9	D
10	B
11	C
12	A
13	A or C
14	D
15	D
16	C

Please See Appendix C for a detailed explanation for each of these answers. Appendix C is written for adults to explain to children how a piece of critical thinking occurred on a problem. Tip: use this review time as a discussion platform on other ways the child may have found the answers.

Numeric Skills

Numeric Skills: Number Series

1.   **14 18 22 26 30 ?**

    a) 51   b) 35   c) 34   d) 62   e) 63

2.   **3 7 11 15 19 ?**

    a) 23   b) 21   c) 24   d) 25   e) 20

3.   **9 13 17 21 25 ?**

    a) 27   b) 31   c) 26   d) 29   e) 30

4.   **24 12 6 ?**

    a) 0   b) 7   c) 3   d) 1   e) 8

5.   **18 21 24 27 ?**

    a) 26   b) 31   c) 29   d) 30   e) 32

6. **16 8 4 ?**
    a) 3   b) 0   c) ②   d) 6   e) 8

7. **4 9 14 19 ?**
    a) 22   b) 34   c) 25   d) 22   e) 24

8. **2 3 5 8 ?**
    a) 12   b) 26   c) 13   d) 25   e) 23

9. **32 16 8 4 ?**
    a) 6   b) 0   c) 8   d) 2   e) 5

10. **3 6 9 12 ?**
    a) 16   b) 17   c) 13   d) 14   e) 15

11. **1 2 4 7 ?**
    a) 9   b) 11   c) 8   d) 14   e) 13

12. **10 15 20 25 30 ?**
    a) 25   b) 45   c) 40   d) 35   e) 32

13. **11 14 17 20 ?**
    a) 20   b) 29   c) 41   d) 33   e) 23

14. <u>1 2 4 7 11 ?</u>

a) 16 b) 12 c) 18 d) 15 e) 14

15. <u>12 10 8 6 ?</u>

a) 5 b) 2 c) 3 d) 1 e) 4

16. <u>1 4 7 10 ?</u>

a) 23 b) 17 c) 11 d) 13 e) 12

17. <u>8 9 11 14 ?</u>

a) 22 b) 18 c) 17 d) 12 e) 16

18. <u>40 20 10 ?</u>

a) 5 b) 6 c) 30 d) 2 e) 4

19. <u>4 5 7 10 ?</u>

a) 15 b) 24 c) 17 d) 19 e) 14

20 <u>11 22 33 ?</u>

a) 45 b) 37 c) 55 d) 44 e) 46

21. <u>8 13 18 23 28 ?</u>

a) 45 b) 48 c) 33 d) 61 e) 44

22. _12   24   36   ?_

   a) 38   b) 48   c) 60   d) 63   e) 47

23. _1   2   4   8   16   ?_

   a) 22   b) 20   c) 34   d) 32   e) 30

24. _121   221   321   ?_

   a) 400   b) 421   c) 333   d) 520   e) 419

25. _10   12   15   17   20   ?_

   a) 22   b) 25   c) 27   d) 21   e) 24

Think Critically

If there are 4 crows on a fence and a goblin throws a rock at one crow and knocks it off the fence, how many crows are there left on the fence?

Answer

There are no crows left on the fence. If one crow gets knocked off the fence the other three will be spooked and fly away.

Number Series: Answer Key

Question	Answer	Question	Answer
1	C	14	C
2	A	15	E
3	D	16	D
4	C	17	B
5	D	18	A
6	C	19	E
7	E	20	D
8	A or C	21	C
9	D	22	B
10	E	23	D
11	B	24	B
12	D	25	A
13	E		

Please See Appendix D for a detailed explanation on how to find these answers and **additional practice**. Appendix D is written for adults to explain to children how a particular piece of critical thinking occurred on a problem. Tip: use this review time as a discussion platform on other ways the child may have found the answers.

Numeric Skills: Number Puzzles

Number Puzzles is a clever way to introduce the student to concepts found in algebra. Here we substitute numbers for shapes and the student must solve a simple math problem given a question with one or more shapes, a math operator (addition or subtraction) and a number that the shape represents. *Tip when you see two or more of the same shape that means to add the number value of those shapes together. For example, if a square is equal to one, two squares next to each other are equal to two.*

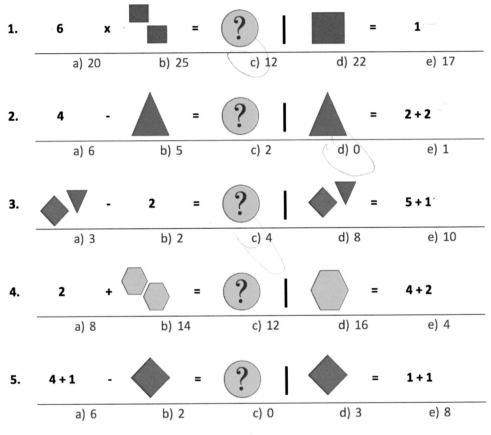

1. 6   x   ⬛⬛ = ? | ⬛ = 1

 a) 20   b) 25   c) 12   d) 22   e) 17

2. 4   -   ▲ = ? | ▲ = 2 + 2

 a) 6   b) 5   c) 2   d) 0   e) 1

3. ◆▼ - 2 = ? | ◆▼ = 5 + 1

 a) 3   b) 2   c) 4   d) 8   e) 10

4. 2   +   ⬡⬡ = ? | ⬡ = 4 + 2

 a) 8   b) 14   c) 12   d) 16   e) 4

5. 4 + 1   -   ◆ = ? | ◆ = 1 + 1

 a) 6   b) 2   c) 0   d) 3   e) 8

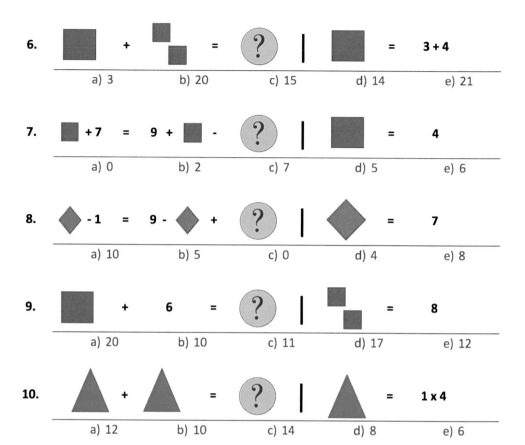

6.   ■ + ◼ = ? | ■ = 3 + 4

    a) 3   b) 20   c) 15   d) 14   e) 21

7.   ■ + 7 = 9 + ■ - ? | ■ = 4

    a) 0   b) 2   c) 7   d) 5   e) 6

8.   ◆ - 1 = 9 - ◆ + ? | ◆ = 7

    a) 10   b) 5   c) 0   d) 4   e) 8

9.   ■ + 6 = ? | ◼ = 8

    a) 20   b) 10   c) 11   d) 17   e) 12

10.   ▲ + ▲ = ? | ▲ = 1 x 4

    a) 12   b) 10   c) 14   d) 8   e) 6

<u>Think Critically</u>
Can you count from 9 to 1 backwards?
(Answer on Next Page)

11. 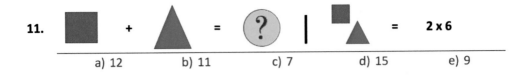 ■ + ▲ = (?) | ■▲ = 2 × 6

a) 12	b) 11	c) 7	d) 15	e) 9

12. 2 × ⬡ = (?) | ⬡ = 7

a) 13	b) 14	c) 28	d) 27	e) 24

13. ◆ - ◆ = (?) | ◆ = ▲

a) 1	b) 2	c) 5	d) 0	e) 9

14. ◆◆ - ◆ + 3 = (?) | ◆ = 8

a) 13	b) 9	c) 12	d) 3	e) 11

15. (?) = ⬡⬡ + ⬡ | ⬡ = 3 + 2 - 4

a) 3	b) 6	c) 8	d) 4	e) 5

Answer
1 2 3 4 5 6 7 8 9
Break the question into 2 parts.
"Can you count from 9 to 1 backwards?"
Part 1: Count from 9 to 1 (9 8 7 6 5 4 3 2 1...)
Part 2: do it backwards (1 2 3 4 5 6 7 8 9)

Number Puzzles: Answer Key

Question	Answer
1	C
2	D
3	C
4	B
5	D
6	E
7	B
8	D
9	B
10	D
11	A
12	B
13	D
14	E
15	A

Please See Appendix E for a detailed explanation for how to find each of these answers. Appendix E is written for adults to explain to children how a piece of critical thinking occurred on a problem. Tip: use this review time as a discussion platform on other ways the child may have found the answers.

Numeric Skills: Number Analogies

1.

20 > 17

18 > 15

17 > ?

26	14	18	29	20
A	B	C	D	E

2.

$$2 > 5$$

$$7 > 10$$

$$5 > \ ?$$

A	B	C	D	E
8	9	18	14	7

3.

| 6 | > | 12 |

| 3 | > | 9 |

| 9 | > | ? |

| 7 | 30 | 15 | 17 | 19 |
| A | B | C | D | E |

4.

| 6 | > | 9 |

| 3 | > | 6 |

| 8 | > | ? |

| 12 | 14 | 9 | 11 | 19 |
| A | B | C | D | E |

5.

2 > 8

3 > 9

10 > ?

23	13	16	17	14
A	B	C	D	E

6.

9 > 14

10 > 15

3 > ?

12	5	16	8	10
A	B	C	D	E

7.

| 12 | > | 6 |

| 10 | > | 5 |

| 8 | > | ? |

| 7 | 9 | 2 | 4 | 6 |
| A | B | C | D | E |

8.

30 > 26

10 > 6

13 > ?

18	8	7	6	9
A	B	C	D	E

9.

5	>	10

4	>	9

3	>	?

8	18	4	6	13
A	B	C	D	E

10.

4 > 8

8 > 12

9 > ?

25	26	13	22	24
(A)	(B)	(C)	(D)	(E)

11.

| 7 | > | 3 |

| 11 | > | 7 |

| 10 | > | ? |

| 5 | 7 | 10 | 9 | 6 |
| A | B | C | D | E |

12.

16 > 15

25 > 24

19 > ?

31	18	17	25	38
A	B	C	D	E

13.

| 2 | > | 6 |

| 4 | > | 8 |

| 10 | > | ? |

| 13 | 22 | 14 | 10 | 16 |
| A | B | C | D | E |

14.

9 > 19

10 > 20

4 > ?

A. 25   B. 15   C. 12   D. 14   E. 21

15.

| 15 | > | 13 |

| 19 | > | 17 |

| 7 | > | ? |

| 6 | 4 | 7 | 5 | 12 |
| A | B | C | D | E |

16.

3	>	23
10	>	30
1	>	?

20	17	40	29	21
A	B	C	D	E

17.

| 2 | > | 4 |

| 4 | > | 8 |

| 3 | > | ? |

| 8 | 6 | 9 | 7 | 13 |
| A | B | C | D | E |

18.

| 18 | > | 11 |

| 15 | > | 8 |

| 11 | > | ? |

| 12 | 7 | 4 | 5 | 9 |
| A | B | C | D | E |

19.

| 10 | > | 5 |

| 12 | > | 6 |

| 4 | > | ? |

| 14 | 0 | 1 | 8 | 2 |
| A | B | C | D | E |

20.

$$3 > 12$$

$$1 > 10$$

$$4 > \; ?$$

(A) 10 (B) 13 (C) 12 (D) 14 (E) 18

Number Analogies: Answer Key

Question	Answer	Question	Answer
1	B	11	E
2	A	12	B
3	C	13	C
4	D	14	D
5	C	15	D
6	D	16	E
7	D	17	B
8	E	18	C
9	A	19	E
10	C	20	B

There is no detailed explanation for this section. In general review with the test taker the answers missed. Tip: In this section there are only four possible patterns. Something is added to each number, something is subtracted from each number, the number is doubling or the number is being cut in half.

Language Skills

Language Skills: Sentence Completion

This section is a standard fill in the blank type of response. Read the question and look for clues as to what the right word is. This isn't a test of how large your vocabulary is, it is more about the clue finding and making an educated guess to the right answer.

1. I felt kind of _____ after I showed up to practice with out any gear and everyone else had theirs. I was afraid the coach would think I wasn't ready to play.
   a) onward   b) awkward   c) embarassing   d) relieved   e) angry

2. Neil Armstrong has _____ so many people to try to become astraunauts. I hope to go to the Moon someday.
   a) taught   b) degraded   c) inspired   d) gave   e) paid

3. The skeleton had us in _____ stuck between flaming nether blocks and a cliff over a pool of lava.
   a) team   b) captivity   c) sights   d) bind   e) doors

4. We tried to _____ with the settlers on the other side of the river by waving our arms towards the bridge.
   a) speak   b) save   c) communicate   d) show   e) trade

5. My dad had to apply for a building _____ before he could put the new pool in our yard. It was easy, costing him only $20.00 and a trip to the city building.
   a) fee   b) document   c) tax   d) permit   e) paper

6. I've been told that the _____ to the modern day dog is actually the grey wolf.
   a) ancestor   b) dad   c) processor   d) mother   e) processor

7. The first nights of the game we had _____ zombie visitors who would
   constantly come by and see if the door was open.
   a) occasional   b) accidental   c) occupational   d) frequent   e) fast

8. Our heroic journey though the mountains came to and end. We slept at the Knights
   Inn and I was glad to be done with all of that _____ .
   a) kinship   b) stewardship   c) hardship   d) pressmanship   e) horsemanship

9. The card was old and _____ , any pressure on it could bend it and any finger prints
   could smudge it forever.
   a) flexible   b) fragile   c) soft   d) hardy   e) hard

10. Your _____ swim times on the 50 meter freestyle have earned you the right to be
    in the State swim meet.
    a) outstanding   b) sidestanding   c) downstanding   d) upstanding   e) instanding

Think Critically

A man is on a trip with a fox, goose, and a sack of corn. He comes upon a stream, which he has
to cross, and finds a tiny boat which he can use. The problem is that he can only take himself
and either the fox, goose, or the corn across at a time. It is not possible for him to leave the fox
alone with the goose (the fox will eat the goose), or the goose alone with the corn (the goose
will eat the corn). How can he get all safely over the stream?

11. **The horse lived in a _____ where it ate at the clovers and grasses.**

   a) swamp   b) mountain   c) house   d) meadow   e) river

12. **The dog _____ all attempts to be friends with it. We gave him treats and bones but it would not come home with us.**

   a) resisted   b) took   c) gave   d) loved   e) received

13. **My uncle was very _____ in letting us stay at his lake house. We would not have been able to afford our own cabin this year.**

   a) garish   b) gordeous   c) hateful   d) gangly   e) generous

14. **The sheep were not all that happy to _____ their wool to the farmer's raw material chest as it was quite cold out.**

   a) burn   b) contribute   c) keep   d) sew   e) wash

15. **A diamond pick axe is _____ because it cuts through stone so fast. Be careful though, it can be burned by lava and it cannot break through bedrock.**

   a) precious   b) porous   c) worthless   d) precarious   e) hard

Answer

The man will take the goose over first and come back. Then he will take the fox, and bring the goose back from the other side. On his next trip, he will take the corn and come back alone to get the goose. Finally, he will take the goose over completing the mission to cross the stream.

16. **The blacksmith was made to _____ nails using iron he had smelted the day before.**

   a) destroy   b) manufacture   c) pick   d) push   e) pull

17. **First get your shovel and some stones in the shape of a cylinder. Then dig a _____ hole to fit the stones into. Lastly, cover the stones with dirt.**

   a) circular   b) pyramid   c) square   d) deep   e) shallow

18. **I chopped at the vine for several minutes and finally it fell from the tree. It was there sitting _____ in front of me no longer attached to the tree.**

   a) stiff   b) down   c) limp   d) upright   e) sitting

19. **The creeper was very _____ having blown up my front door and the wall to my house.**

   a) deplorable   b) demanding   c) destructive   d) daring   e) friendly

20. **It wasn't _____ to run in the halls so I walked like normal.**

   a) sad   b) appropriate   c) rule   d) poor   e) great

End Of Section!
Keep Up The Good Work!

Sentence Completion: Answer Key

Question	Answer	Question	Answer
1	B	11	D
2	C	12	A
3	B	13	E
4	C	14	B
5	D	15	A
6	A	16	B
7	D	17	A
8	C	18	C
9	B	19	C
10	A	20	B

There is no detailed explanation for this section. In general review with the test taker the answers missed. Tips:

- Review each answer in a question and try to force yourself to pick from the top two answers. This will help make sure you have considered each question thoroughly.
- The elimination method works for this section just as you did for the visual problems in previous sections.

Language Skills: Verbal Classification

Questions in this section will show you three words that are related in a certain way. Pick a word from the set of answers that are also related in that same certain way. To say it another way, you will be classifying the words, maybe they are items in a kitchen or things that you do or types of food. When you figure out the classification, choose a word from the answers that most closely fits that classification.

1. **England**   **Germany**   **Italy**   _____
   a) Russia   b) America   c) Mexico
   d) Brazil   e) France

2. **Canada**   **Iceland**   **Alaska**   _____
   a) Greenland   b) Brazil   c) China
   d) South Africa e) France

3. **Africa**   **Antatctica**   **Europe**   _____
   a) Germany   b) Asia   c) America
   d) Russia   e) Greenland

4. **lagoon**   **lake**   **pond**   _____
   a) falls   b) rapids   c) river
   d) swamp   e) stream

5. **balance**   **buy**   **blanket**   _____
   a) capital   b) note   c) cheap
   d) barry   e) coupon

6. **cartoon** **animation** **painting** _____
   a) portrait b) comic c) portray
   d) oil paint e) watercolor

7. **CD** **keyboard** **mouse** _____
   a) joystick b) WWW c) web page
   d) surf e) backup

8. **chair** **table** **sofa** _____
   a) couch b) rug c) fireplace
   d) lamp e) painting

9. **battle axe** **spear** **sword** _____
   a) horse b) lance c) shield
   d) armor e) catapault

10. **village** **town** **metropolis** _____
    a) city b) Dalas c) New York
    d) Florida e) community

11. **square**   **diamond**   **rhombus**   _____

a) trapezoid   b) pentagram   c) shapes

d) triangle   e) circle

12. **zebra**   **dog**   **cat**   _____

a) lion   b) butterfly   c) furry

d) animals   e) ant

13. **rapids**   **falls**   **stream**   _____

a) swamp   b) pond   c) river

d) lake   e) lagoon

14. **baron**   **prince**   **duke**   _____

a) castle   b) earl   c) kingdom

d) royalty   e) manor

15. **father**   **mother**   **brother**   _____

a) sister   b) cousin   c) grandparent

d) uncle   e) son

16. **aunt**   **mother**   **wife**   _____
    a) father   b) nephew   c) sister
    d) brother   e) uncle

17. **stone**   **drawbridge**   **moat**   _____
    a) nobility   b) dungeon   c) battle axe
    d) king   e) fly

18. **ham**   **bacon**   **sausage**   _____
    a) mustard   b) bun   c) hamburger
    d) cola   e) celery

19. **Florida**   **Alabama**   **North Carolina** _____
    a) Mexico   b) America   c) New York
    d) Germany   e) Asia

20. **dragster**   **limo**   **coupe**   _____
    a) car   b) cruiser   c) motorcycle
    d) bike   e) 4 wheel drive

Think Critically

An old wooden sail ship called "Athens" takes a voyage around the world. As the ship sails around to each port the sailors must make repairs. One by one each piece of the ship is replaced for a newer part. 20 years later the ship has returned to its home with every piece of the ship replaced. Is it the same ship?

21.	**hair brush**	**tooth brush**	**soap**	_____
	a) table	b) coat hanger	c) chair	
	d) mirror	e) microwave		

22.	**buoy**	**crows nest**	**plank**	_____
	a) naval	b) sailor	c) motorboat	
	d) sail	e) ship		

23.	**coal**	**wind**	**solar**	_____
	a) oil	b) energy	c) kilowatt	
	d) waste	e) windmill		

24.	**tornado**	**hurricane**	**hail**	_____
	a) clouds	b) wind	c) precipitation	
	d) climate	e) thunder		

25.	**Mercury**	**Venus**	**Earth**	_____
	a) moon	b) Mars	c) comet	
	d) Sun	e) asteroid		

Answer

There is no right answer! This is a philosophy question called a paradox. If you said it was a new ship now ask yourself exactly when did the ship become 'a new ship'. Was it when the first repair was made? Or was it when the very last piece of the ship was replaced? If you said it is still the same ship, how can you say that if every part of the old ship was replaced?

Verbal Classification: Answer Key

Question	Answer	Question	Answer
1	B	14	B
2	A	15	A
3	B	16	A
4	D	17	B
5	D	18	C
6	B	19	C
7	A	20	B
8	A	21	D
9	B	22	D
10	A	23	E
11	A	24	B
12	A	25	B
13	C		

There is no appendix for Verbal Classification explaining the correct answers. Please review the answer sheet here and have a discussion on which questions were missed and what the correct answer is.

Language Skills: Verbal Analogies

This section has the familiar, "this word" is to "that word" as "other word" is to "[pick a word]". The only difference is the related words are separated by a |----------| instead of linking with the 'is to' 'as' words as you have probably seen before. So look at the first two words presented, figure out their relation, then look at the next word and pick a word from the answer set that has that same relation.

1.   mother |----------| female
         rock |----------| _____

   a) wood   b) hard   c) sharp
   d) dangerous   e) green

2.   salty |----------| bacon
        sweet |----------| _____

   a) bread   b) beef   c) candy
   d) sound   e) cola

3.   nose |----------| aroma
         eye |----------| _____

   a) sight   b) haze   c) taste
   d) smell   e) mist

4.   paper clip |----------| fasten
         knife |----------| _____

   a) tool   b) draw   c) metal
   d) sharp   e) cut

5.   dish |----------| dish soap
         hand |----------| _____

   a) bar soap   b) hand soap   c) liquid soap
   d) car soap   e) laundry soap

6.   meal |----------| breakfast
               bed |----------| _____

a) sleep   b) crib   c) mother
d) couch   e) sheet

7.   nice |----------| unkind
             hideous |----------| _____

a) pretty   b) awful   c) safe
d) noisy   e) angry

8.   hurricane |----------| storm
                chair |----------| _____

a) furnature   b) wind   c) wood
d) table   e) rain

9.   unknown |----------| fame
              ignorant |----------| _____

a) child   b) manners   c) education
d) boy   e) school

10.   televion |----------| watch
                 book |----------| _____

a) watch   b) read   c) listen
d) comic   e) novel

11.   weak |----------| strong
             brave |----------| _____

a) friends   b) coward   c) silly

d) lost   e) courage

12.   big |----------| giant
               fast |----------| _____

a) run   b) quick   c) slow

d) tiny   e) small

13.   meat |----------| bacon
            drink |----------| _____

a) ham   b) fizzy   c) candy

d) cola   e) beef

14.   fisherman |----------| hook
         gardener |----------| _____

a) shovel   b) hat   c) seed

d) glove   e) weed

15.   dim |----------| faint
           chilly |----------| _____

a) snow   b) cold   c) hail

d) ice   e) winter

16.
penny |----------| coin
pants |----------| _____

a) soft   b) cloth   c) jacket
d) shirt   e) clothing

17.
mountain |----------| high
valley |----------| _____

a) lonely   b) wet   c) green
d) low   e) river

18.
baker |----------| bread
carpender |----------| _____

a) hammer   b) nails   c) chairs
d) tool belt   e) wood

19.
cake |----------| dessert
throne |----------| _____

a) queen   b) castle   c) chairs
d) prince   e) fortress

20.
tiredness |----------| sleep
curiosity |----------| _____

a) look   b) run   c) exploration
d) rest   e) write

21.   page |----------| book
            tree |----------| _____

a) timber   b) forrest   c) bushes
d) plant   e) wood

22.   helicopter |----------| sky
        submarine |----------| _____

a) street   b) water   c) dives
d) boat   e) float

23.   gold |----------| expensive
            velvet |----------| _____

a) dull   b) hard   c) brown
d) raw   e) soft

24.   shovel |----------| dig
              pen |----------| _____

a) ink   b) pencil   c) write
d) paper   e) crayon

End Of Section!
Keep Up The Good Work!

Verbal Analogies: Answer Key

Question	Answer	Question	Answer
1	B	13	D
2	C	14	A
3	A	15	B
4	E	16	E
5	B	17	D
6	B	18	C
7	A	19	C
8	A	20	C
9	C	21	B
10	B	22	B
11	B	23	E
12	B	24	C

There is no appendix for Verbal Analogies explaining the correct answers. Please review the answer sheet here and have a discussion on which questions were missed and what the correct answer is.

Appendix A: Figure Classification Answer Guide

Here we explain each question and answer found in the Figure Classification quiz. The answer is found in the text under the question.

Figure Classification: Question 1

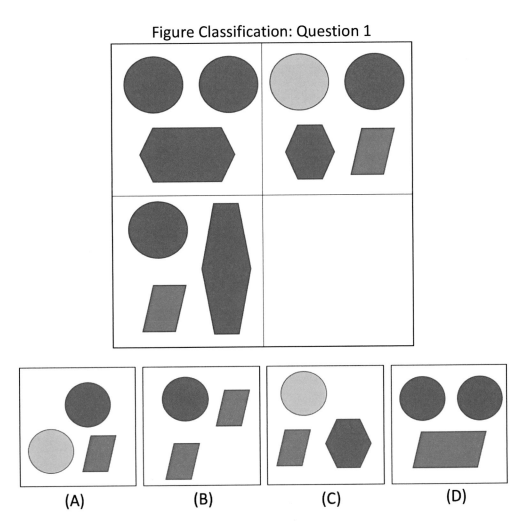

(A) (B) (C) (D)

Answer C is our selection for this question. Each sample picture has a hexagon, answer C is the only answer with a hexagon. We also see pictures with an orange circle and a red diamond so we know these shapes are ok as well.

Figure Classification: Question 2

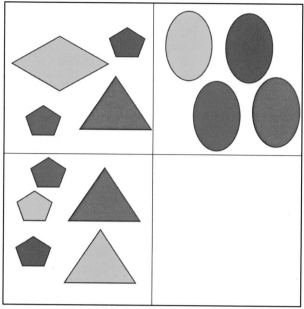

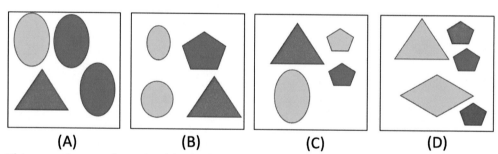

(A) (B) (C) (D)

This question can be solved by looking at the colors. All of the example squares contain at least one red, yellow, blue, and green shape. Only D has all 4 colors, so it is the correct answer.

Figure Classification: Question 3

(A)   (B)   (C)   (D)

This question could be based on the number of shapes or the color. We can see that each square has a yellow, blue, green and red shape. In the answers, only C has a shape of each color. However, there are 2 green shapes instead of one. The other possibility is that each square has 4 total items. In our answers, all of them have 5 items except for B which has 4. The best answer is B because it has 4 shapes like the squares. You could argue that it should be C, based on the colors, but B is the better answer because if we look at the colors, C has 2 green instead of 1.

Figure Classification: Question 4

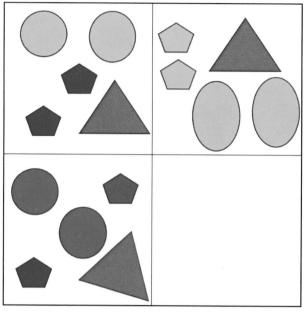

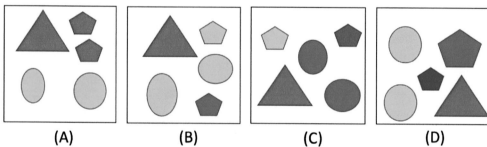

| (A) | (B) | (C) | (D) |

In this example, all of the squares and answers have 2 circles, 2 pentagons, and a triangle. So the next thing we look at is color. In every square, the circles match color and so do the pentagons. When we look at the answers, we see that only answer A has circles and pentagons that are of the same color. Answer A is correct.

Figure Classification: Question 5

(A) (B) (C) (D)

This question is based on shapes. Every square has 2 pentagons, 2 circles, and a triangle. If we look at our answers, only answer D has 2 circles, 2 pentagons, and a triangle. Answer D is correct.

Figure Classification: Question 6

(A) (B) (C) (D)

We need to solve this one by eliminating options to get the best answer. We should eliminate D first because although it has 2 triangles and a circle like some of our squares, they are all blue while the example squares have different colors. C could fit because it has 2 blue triangles like the first square. A and B look like they could fit, but we should choose C over them because the circle is red, and in our examples the circle is always blue. C is the best answer because it has 2 blue triangles like the first square.

Figure Classification: Question 7

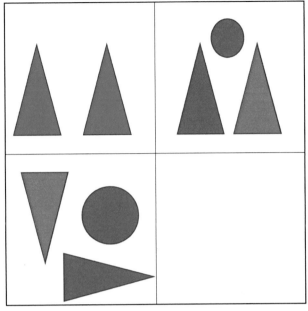

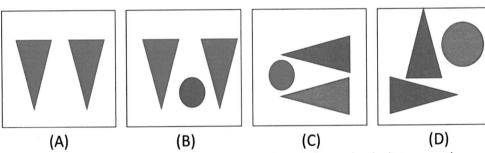

(A)　　　　　　　(B)　　　　　　　(C)　　　　　　　(D)

The color scheme of the example squares with a circle are both the same; they both have a red triangle, a blue triangle, and a blue circle. When looking at the answers, B, C, and D all have a different color scheme. This means that A is the best answer because it has 2 green triangles like the first square.

Figure Classification: Question 8

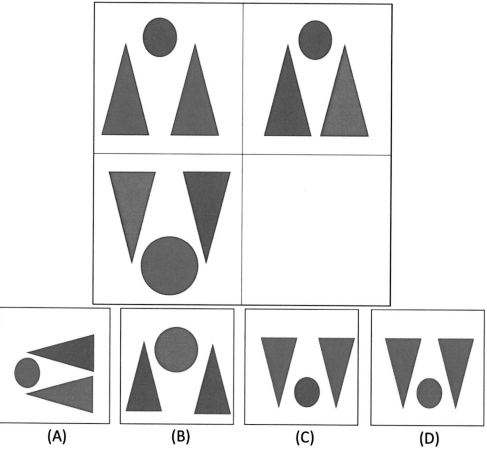

(A)   (B)   (C)   (D)

Answer A can be eliminated because it is pointing a different direction than all of the examples. Answer D can be eliminated because it is all the same color. Is the answer B or C? C is the better answer because it is just the reverse of the first square, and is facing the same direction as the bottom square.

Figure Classification: Question 9

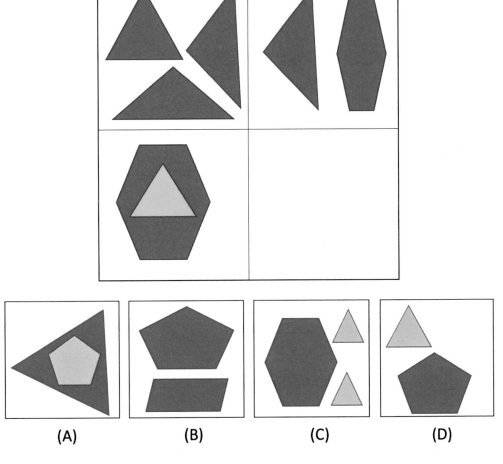

(A) (B) (C) (D)

This question is based on the total number of sides. All of the example of 9 total sides. The first one has 3 triangles, which is 9 total sides, the second has a triangle and a hexagon, which is 9, and the third one has the same except they are positioned differently and have a different color to try to throw you off. The correct answer is B, which is a 4 sided and a 5 sided shape for 9 total sides.

Figure Classification: Question 10

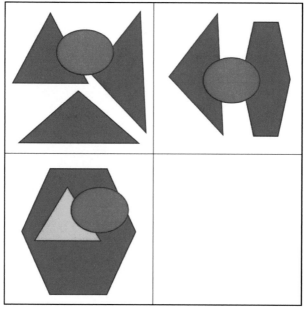

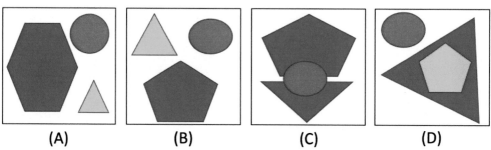

(A)   (B)   (C)   (D)

The best answer here is C, because the red circle is on top of the shapes like in all of the example squares.

Figure Classification: Question 11

(A)   (B)   (C)   (D)

The common thing among these squares is that they all have 3 different shapes of 3 different colors. A is the only answer that fits those criteria.

Figure Classification: Question 12

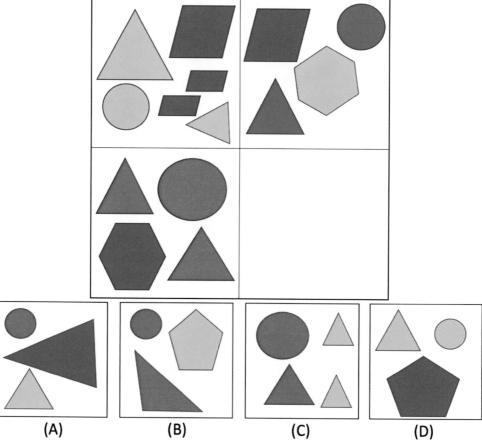

(A)   (B)   (C)   (D)

The Answer here is B or D. In the above pictures the triangle's color always matches the color of the circle. The other shapes are just noise in the question.

Figure Classification: Question 13

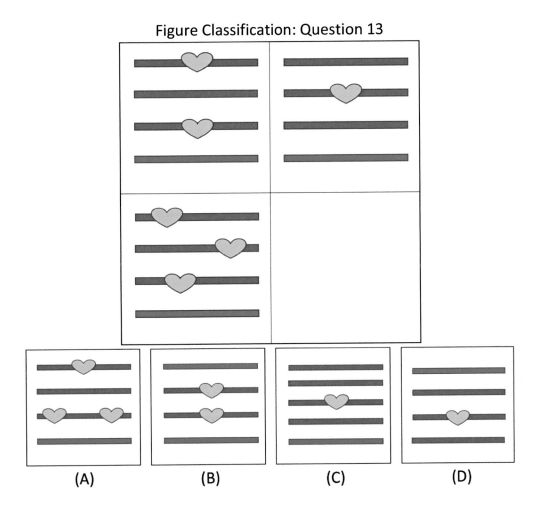

(A)   (B)   (C)   (D)

In this question only the line numbers and colors end up being important. All of the squares have 3 blue lines followed by a green line. That means that A is the answer because it is the only one that matches.

Figure Classification: Question 14

(A)   (B)   (C)   (D)

We can narrow down the correct answer to C or D based on the number of lines and the color scheme. Between C and D, D is the best answer because it has hearts on 2 lines, which is the maximum number of lines that have hearts in the squares.

Figure Classification: Question 15

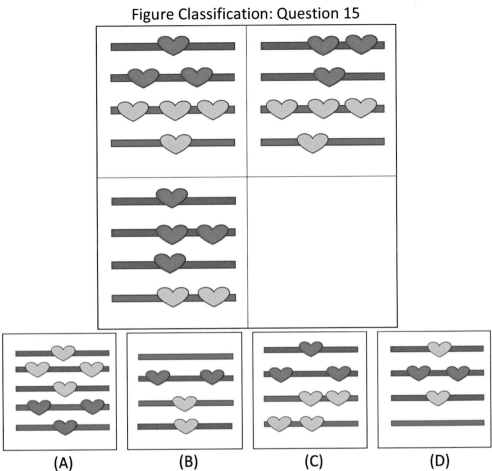

(A)	**(B)**	**(C)**	**(D)**

Once again we can eliminate A easily because it has too many lines. B can also be eliminated because it has green lines in different places than the squares.
Between C and D, C is the best answer because D has too few hearts compared to the example squares.

Figure Classification: Question 16

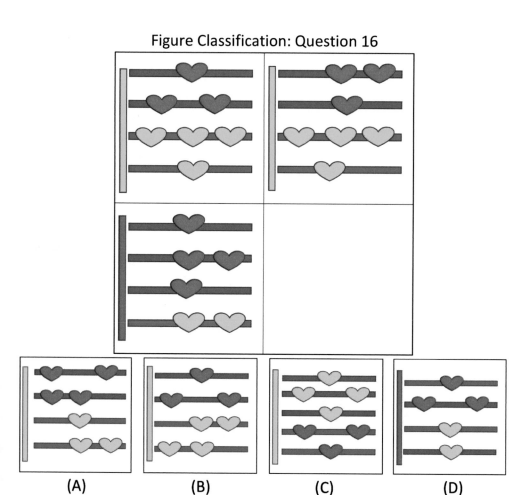

(A) (B) (C) (D)

A and B are very similar answers. C and D should be eliminated because the lines are either a different color scheme or there are too many. Between A and B, B is the best answer because it has 4 yellow hearts whereas A has 3 yellow hearts. No examples have 3 yellow hearts, so B is the correct answer.

Figure Classification: Question 17

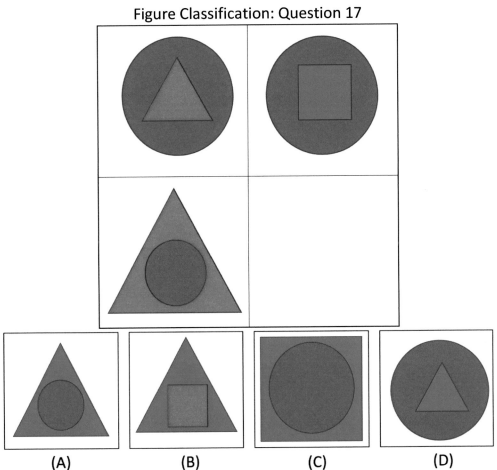

The first thing to notice in these squares is that all circles are blue. That eliminates answer B. The triangles in our examples are red, and if we follow this logic that eliminates A and D. Answer C has a blue circle and a green square, which matches our example. C is the answer.

Figure Classification: Question 18

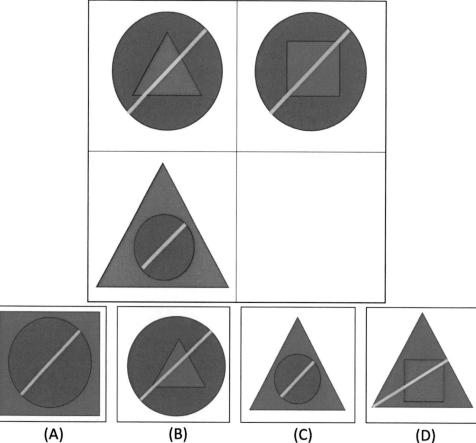

(A)   (B)   (C)   (D)

In the example squares the yellow line stretches across the circle. This eliminates answer D. If we look at the color, scheme, answer A is the best answer because it has the reverse of the second square; it has a green square with a blue circle in it.

Figure Classification: Question 19

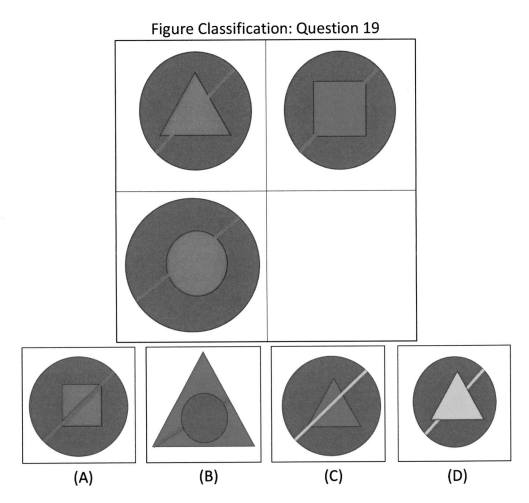

(A)   (B)   (C)   (D)

In all of the example squares the line matches the color of the shape that it goes across.
D is the only answer that will work because it has a yellow line through a yellow triangle.

Figure Classification: Question 20

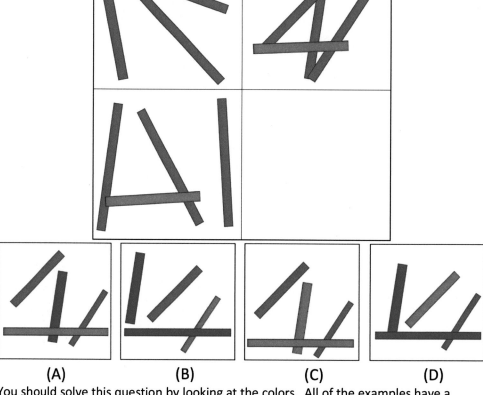

(A)   (B)   (C)   (D)

You should solve this question by looking at the colors. All of the examples have a horizontal red rectangle which means our answer should be A or C. We can eliminate answer C because it has 2 red shapes and 2 blue shapes, while all of the examples have 3 blue shapes and 1 red shape. That means that A is the correct answer.

Appendix B: Figure Matrices Answer Guide
Figure Matrices: Question 1

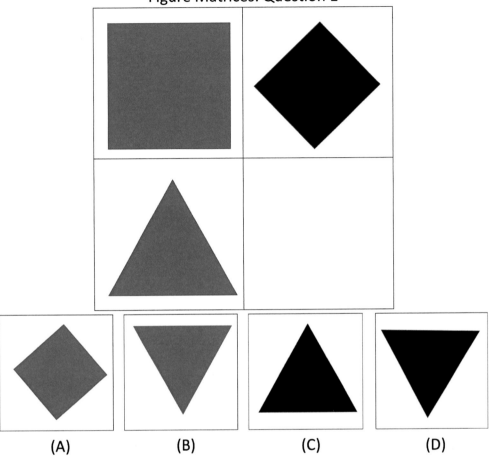

(A)   (B)   (C)   (D)

In this example the square rotates and turns black. The only answer that has a rotated triangle that turns black is D, so the answer is D.

Figure Matrices: Question 2

(A)   (B)   (C)   (D)

The triangle turns in to 3 triangles – one pointed up and 2 pointed down. On the bottom, we are looking for 3 pentagons with one pointed up and 2 pointed down. The answer is D.

Figure Matrices: Question 3

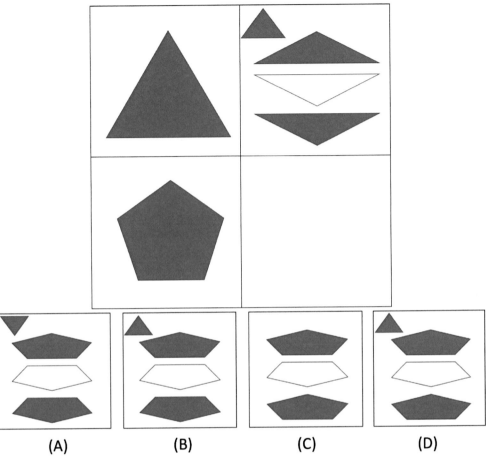

(A)   (B)   (C)   (D)

A triangle turns in to 4 triangles. Follow the same pattern for the pentagon on the bottom and you get the answer is B. The pentagon turns in to 2 pentagons pointing down (one white) and one pointing up, and has an added small triangle.

Figure Matrices: Question 4

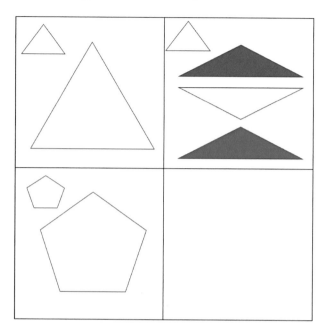

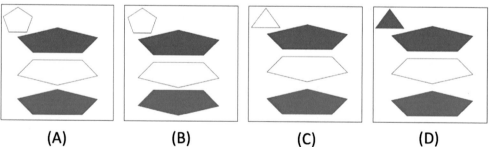

(A)   (B)   (C)   (D)

For this one we can see that a small pentagon should stay in the top left hand corner. That eliminates answers C and D. A and B are the same except for the direction of the green pentagon, and if we look at the top example we can see that the shape should be pointed up. That means that A is the answer.

Figure Matrices: Question 5

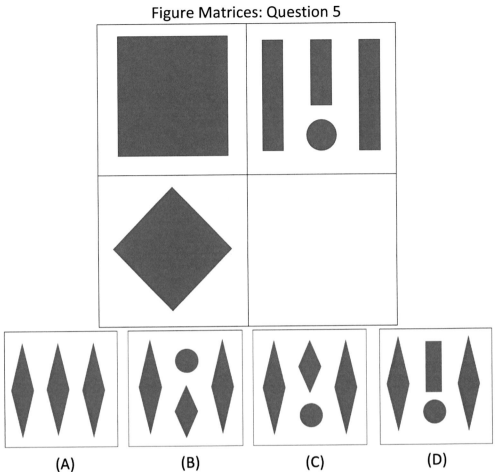

(A)   (B)   (C)   (D)

The square turns in to 3 squished squares (rectangles) with a circle in the middle on the bottom. The correct answer is C because it has the small diamond in the center top and the circle in the center bottom.

Figure Matrices: Question 6

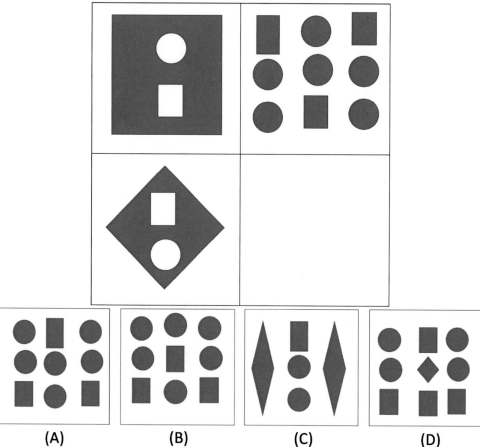

There are a lot of shapes here, but what is happening is the white shapes staying in the middle and are turning blue, and an additional circle is added on the top. Then the blue rectangle is going to the top left and top right with additional circles underneath. So in the bottom, we should expect the white shapes to stay in the middle, turn blue, and add an additional circle on the bottom. That narrows it down to A or C. A is correct because C only has a single long shape on the sides.

Figure Matrices: Question 7

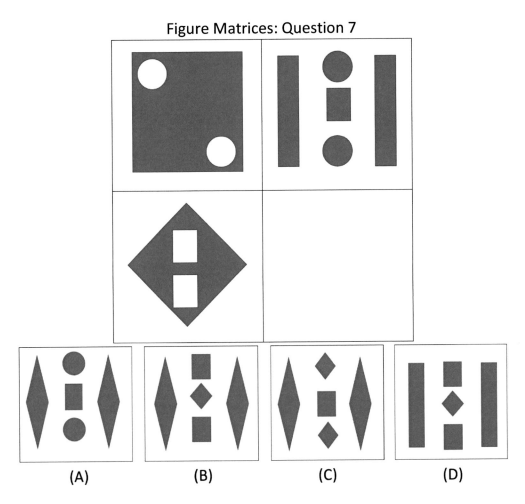

(A)   (B)   (C)   (D)

The blue square is being turn in to 2 blue rectangles on either side, and a small blue rectangle in the middle. On the bottom we have a large blue diamond, so we can expect to have diamonds on the side and in the middle for the answer. The only answer that has that is B.

Figure Matrices: Question 8

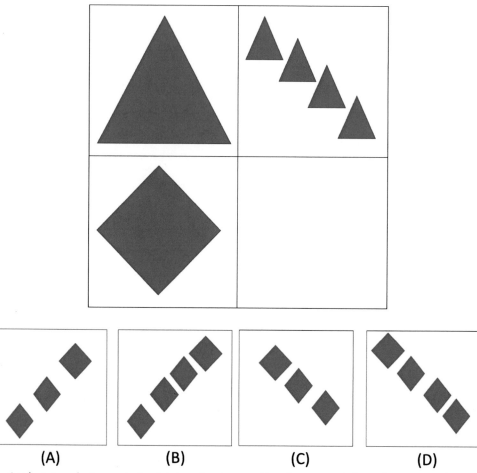

(A)   (B)   (C)   (D)

A single triangle turns in to 4 triangle descending from top left to bottom right. D is the correct answer because it has 4 diamonds in the same descending order.

Figure Matrices: Question 9

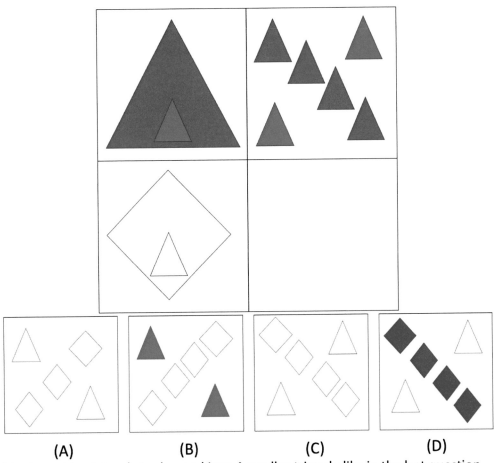

(A)   (B)   (C)   (D)

The large blue triangle is changed into 4 smaller triangle like in the last question, but not the small green triangle is now moved into both the bottom left and top right corner. For the answer, we should see 4 descending diamonds and then a triangle in the bottom left and top right corner. C is the correct answer.

Figure Matrices: Question 10

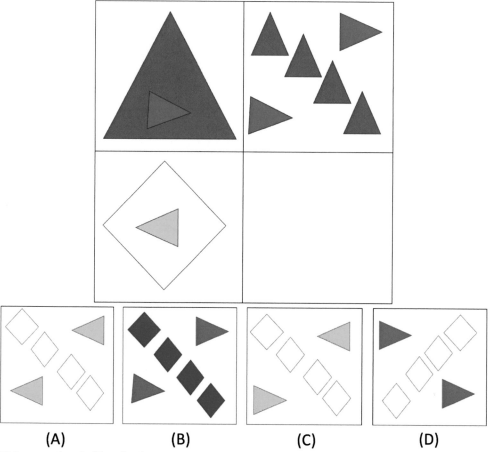

(A)   (B)   (C)   (D)

This question is like the last one except the triangle is pointed a different direction. A is the correct answer because the triangles are pointed the same direction as the example square.

Figure Matrices: Question 11

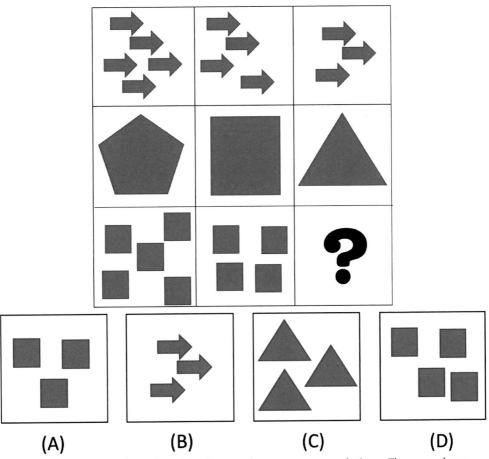

(A)   (B)   (C)   (D)

This question involves subtraction. The first row loses an arrow each time. The second row keeps losing a side on the shape. In the last row, we should expect 3 squares. The answer is A.

Figure Matrices: Question 12

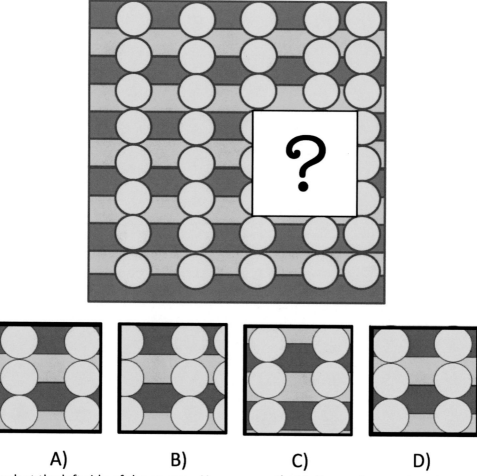

A)   B)   C)   D)

Look at the left side of the square. You can see that is it covering up almost an entire column of circles. In your answer you should see almost an entire circle on the left, but it should be cut off on the left. Only B matches, so it is the correct answer.

Figure Matrices: Question 13

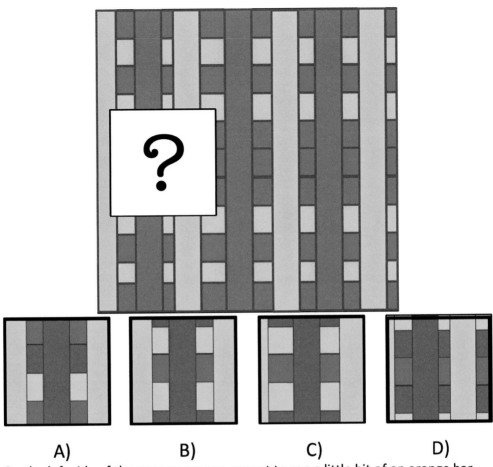

A)   **B)**   **C)**   **D)**

On the left side of the answer we can expect to see a little bit of an orange bar.
That narrows down the answer to C or D. If you look at the bottom of those 2
answers, one has a horizontal blue bar and the other is orange. If we look at the ?
box, we see that we should expect a slim orange bar on the bottom. D is correct.

Figure Matrices: Question 14

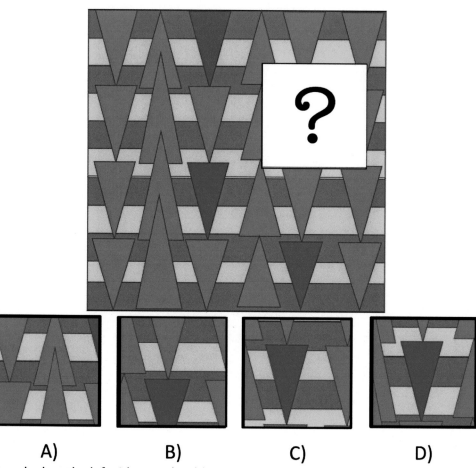

A)   B)   C)   D)

If we look at the left side, we should expect to see about half of a single green triangle pointing up. C and D both kind of fit this, so we can next compare the right side, where we should expect to see about half of a green triangle pointing down. The answer is C.

Figure Matrices: Question 15

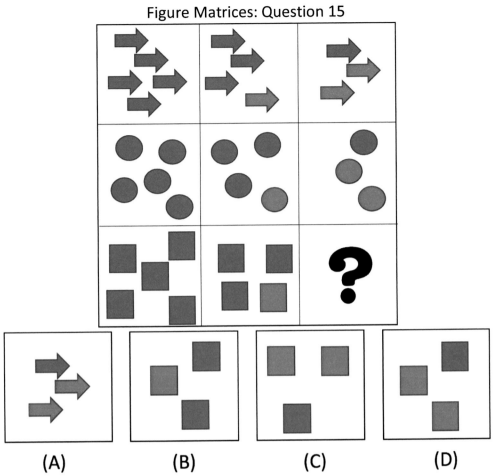

(A)   (B)   (C)   (D)

In each square across the row, we subtract a shape and turn a shape red starting from the bottom up. D is the correct answer because it has 2 red squares on the bottom.

Figure Matrices: Question 16

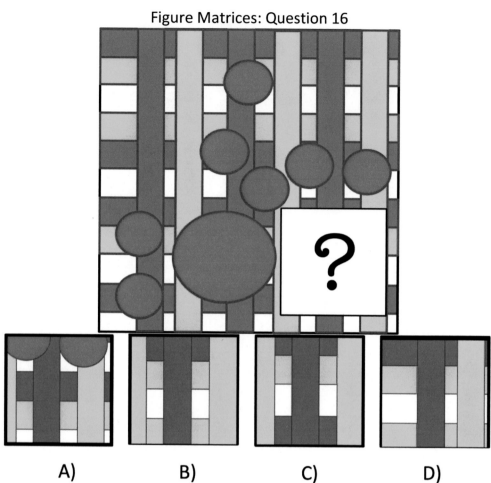

A)   B)   C)   D)

For this question let's look at the horizontal bars. We should have part of a blue line on top, then an orange line, and then a blue line on the bottom. The only answer that works is C.

Figure Matrices: Question 17

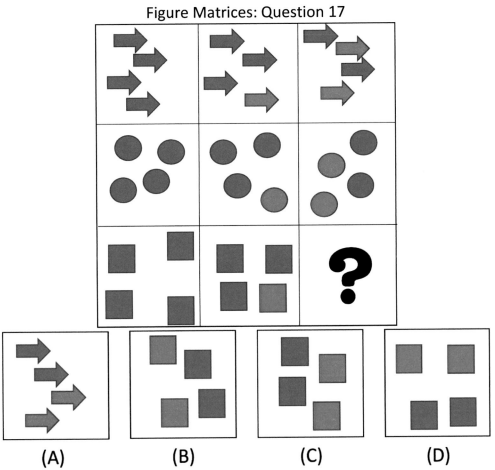

(A) (B) (C) (D)

In these examples, the second column turns a blue item red on the right side. Then, in the third column, there are 2 red items on the left. The best answer is B because it perfectly matches the second row, which has 2 red items on the left side.

Figure Matrices: Question 18

A)   B)   C)   D)

In this question the location of the items is important. D is the best answer because the squares are aligned in the same locations as in the second row, and they have the correct color scheme.

Figure Matrices: Question 19

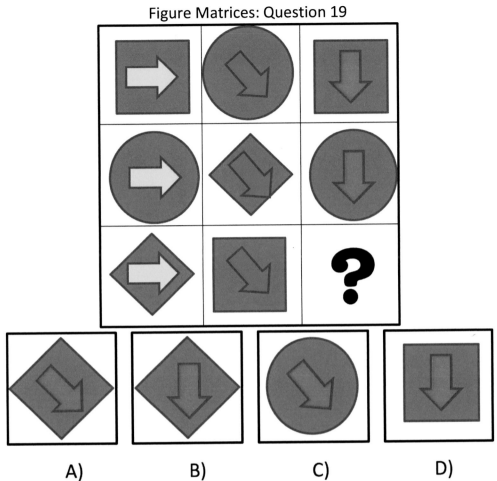

The first thing you can do is eliminate answers A and C because the arrow is not pointing in the correct direction. In the examples, the third column always has an arrow pointing straight down. Next, notice that the first and third columns have the same blue shape. In the bottom example, it starts with a diamond shape which means that the correct answer is B.

Figure Matrices: Question 20

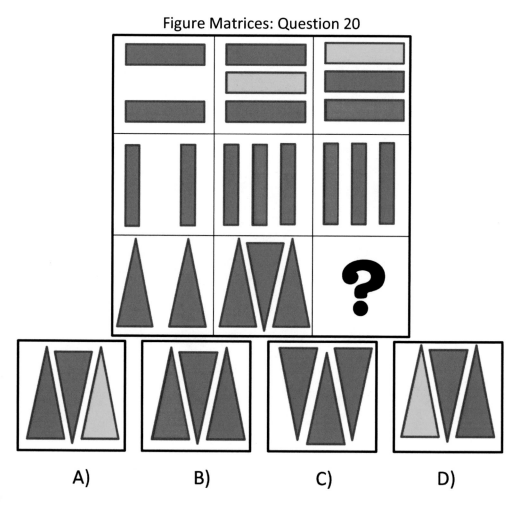

A)   B)   C)   D)

The pattern in this question is that a different color and an additional shape are added in the second column, and then then another color is added in the third column. We can eliminate answer C because the triangles are only of 2 different colors, but how can we choose between A, B, and D? The best information we have is in the second row; We see a red shape, a blue shape and a green shape. This same pattern is seen in answer B.

Figure Matrices: Question 21 (Bonus)

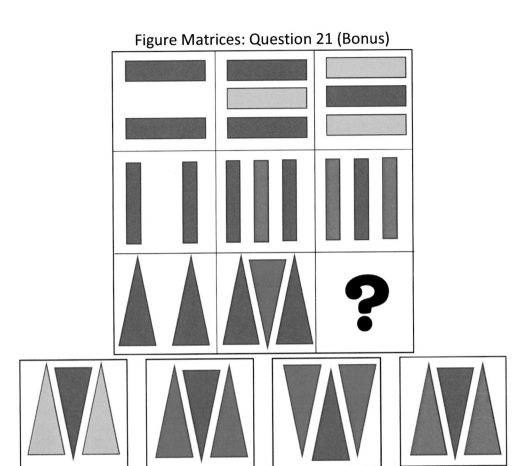

(A)   (B)   (C)   (D)

In this question the color that is added in the second column then moves to the outsides in the third column. So we should expect green to be on the outsides. Is B or C correct? B is the best answer because we see that the triangles on the outsides stay pointing up.

Figure Matrices: Question 22 (Bonus)

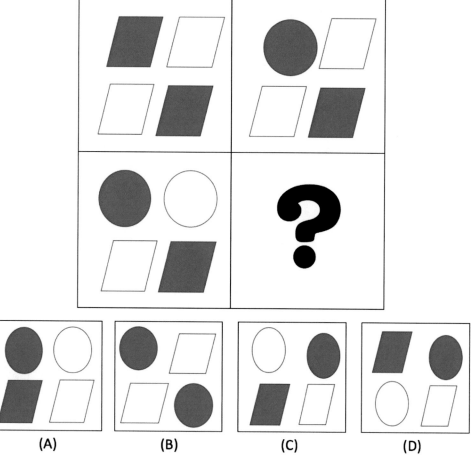

(A)   (B)   (C)   (D)

Each picture here shows blue and white shapes. The blue shapes are always top left and bottom right and the white shapes are always top right and bottom left. Answer B is the only one with this characteristic.

The idea that there may be 0, 1 or 2 circles is just there to throw you off the real answer.

Figure Matrices: Question 23 (Bonus)

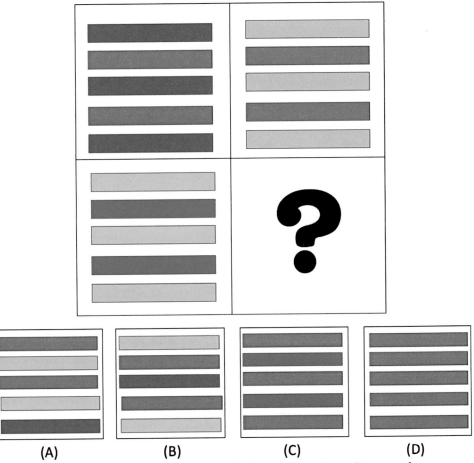

(A)　　　　　(B)　　　　　(C)　　　　　(D)

Each shape presented has exactly two colors and the colors alternate from one to the other. Kind of like boy-girl-boy-girl seating. Answer C is the only answer that has two colors that alternate.

Figure Matrices: Question 24 (Bonus)

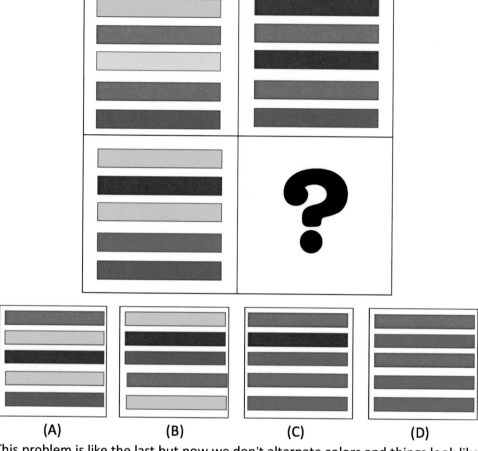

(A)   (B)   (C)   (D)

This problem is like the last but now we don't alternate colors and things look like a mess.

Investigate each shape and ask yourself "What is similar among these shapes?"

Each shape has a blue line on the bottom. Answer A has a blue line on the bottom, all other answers do not.

It is ok to struggle with this one. You are training to drown out the noise and try to find what is important to each picture.

Figure Matrices: Question 25 (Bonus)

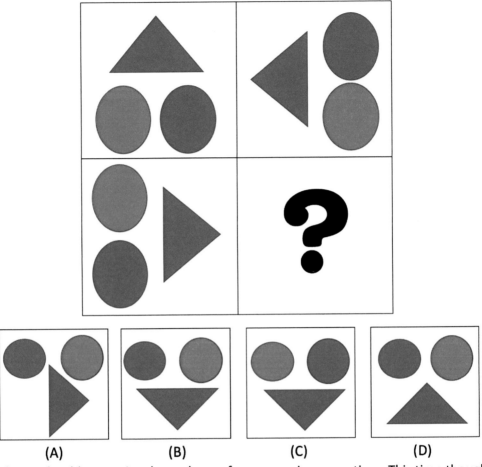

(A)   (B)   (C)   (D)

Ok you should recognize these shapes from a previous question. This time though we have introduced red shapes into the mix. The answer is B. Can you figure out why? Let's do elimination. In each sample the triangle points away from the circles. Answer A and D are out!

So we have left B and C which only look different in where the red circle is placed. To figure this out take any one of the pictures presented and 'rotate' the whole picture so that the triangle is pointing down. When you do this you should see the red circle should be on the right side when the triangle is pointing down.

Answer C is out and Answer B is the winner.

Appendix C: Paper Folding Answer Guide
Paper Folding: Question 1

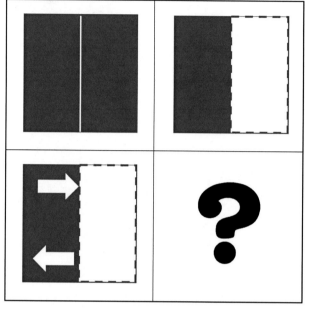

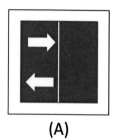
(A)

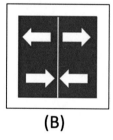
(B)

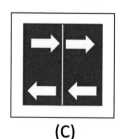
(C)

(D)

Question one starts out with a paper being folded in half and then arrows pointing right and left are punched. When unfolded what will the piece of paper look like? The important thing here is to think of the paper halves as mirrors. The arrows will flip from the way they are pointing now. The top arrow points right and when the paper is unfolded the two top arrows will point towards each other. The bottom arrow will flip and the two arrows will point away from each other. Answer D shows the arrows pointing in the proper way.

Paper Folding: Question 2

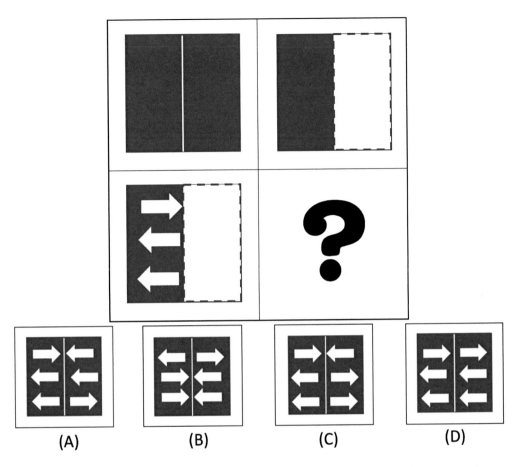

(A)   (B)   (C)   (D)

This question is a play off of question 1 with three arrows to consider. Here the top arrows when unfolded will point towards each other and the bottom two arrows will become four arrows pointing away from each other. Answer C is the winner.

Paper Folding: Question 3

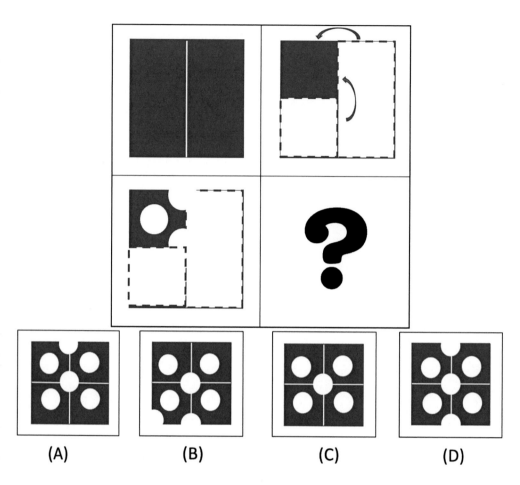

(A)   (B)   (C)   (D)

Moving from arrows and half sheets we now look at circles and a quarter sheet. The paper is folded twice and three holes are punched. Think of this in two parts. What will the paper look like when unfolded once? Then what will the paper look like when unfolded twice? The giveaway here is that top ¼ circle punched in the sheet. When it is unfolded you should see part of a circle punched out of the top AND bottom of the sheet. Only answer D has this kind of mark.

Paper Folding: Question 4

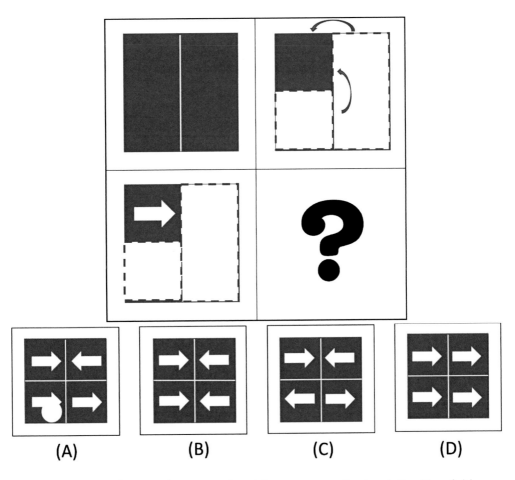

(A)   (B)   (C)   (D)

Think again on unfolding this one twice. The arrow on the top left will unfold once showing two arrows on the left pointing to the right. Then when it is unfolded again you'll get the flip. You should see two arrows pointing right and two arrows pointing left. Answer B shows this.

Paper Folding: Question 5

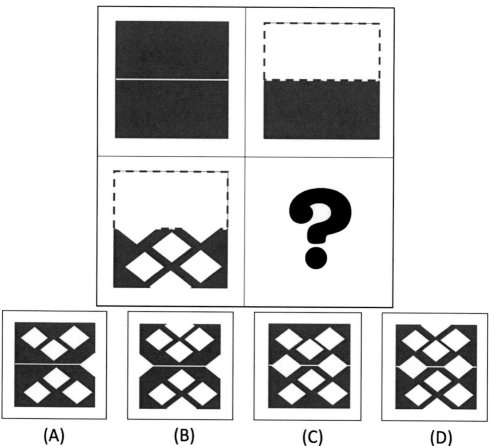

(A)   (B)   (C)   (D)

This one has a lot of shapes. Lets use the elimination method for this question. In the fold we see two half diamond shapes cut on the centerline. Answers A and B do not have these same shapes on the centerline. So we pick from answers C and D. What's different from C and D? D has those half diamonds cut out on the top and bottom. Is that more or less correct than C when compared to the cutout in the question? The question shows a half diamond cutout on the bottom of the paper so that looks more correct. Answer D is the winner.

Paper Folding: Question 6

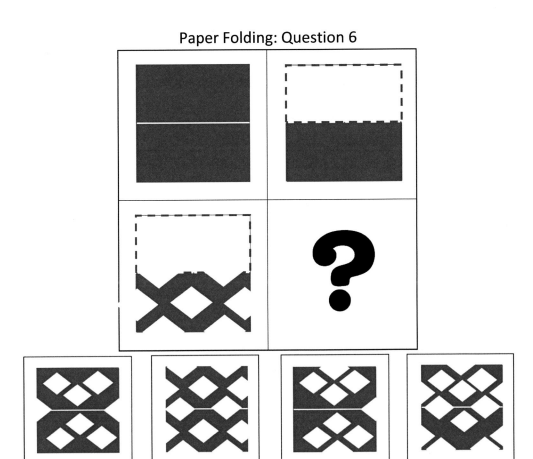

(A)   (B)   (C)   (D)

Now lets use the concept of negative space to solve a question. Instead of looking at the purple part of the cutout relax your eyes and focus on the white part. It looks like a pattern of repeating diamonds. So which answer has that same pattern of repeating diamonds on the bottom and top when unfolded? The Answer is B. The other answers do not show the same pattern.

Paper Folding: Question 7

173

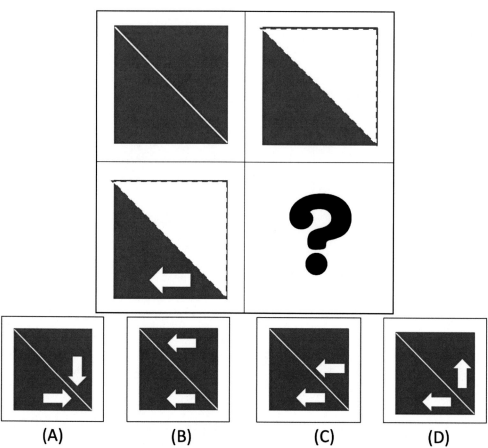

(A)   (B)   (C)   (D)

Arrows on diagonally folded paper can be tricky. Instead of flipping, the arrows will rotate. The arrow is pointing towards the left but as the paper is unfolded along the diagonal line the second arrow will be pointing up. Compare answer B to answer D. The arrow at the bottom can't get all the way to the top of the page like answer B, instead it will just kind of rotate like in answer D.

Paper Folding: Question 8

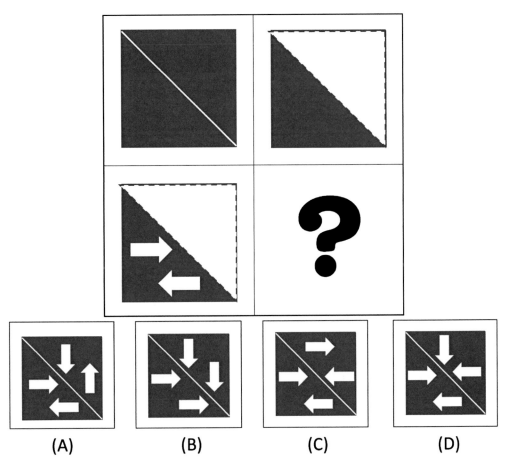

(A)   (B)   (C)   (D)

This is the same question but with another arrow. We already know how that bottom arrow will play out. It will become two arrows; the second arrow will be pointing up. Looking at all of the answers we see that A is the only one that correctly handles the bottom arrow. It is a giveaway. Answer A also handles the other arrow correctly so do review how that looks before going on.

Paper Folding: Question 9

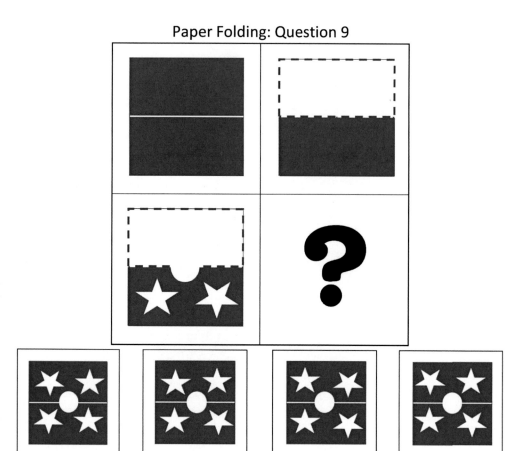

(A)   (B)   (C)   (D)

Now more complex shapes. Think of these stars like you think of the arrows. The stars will flip along that fold line. Answer D shows this flip with the left star the point of the star is pointing towards the centerline for both stars after the fold.

Paper Folding: Question 10

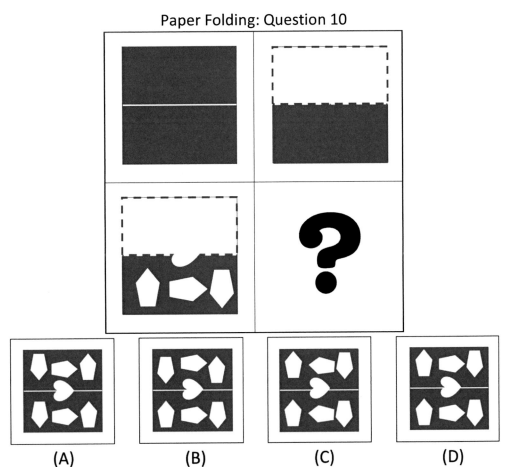

(A)   (B)   (C)   (D)

More different shapes for question 10. As with any shape that isn't a circle, try to treat it like an arrow. The pentagon on the left is pointing towards the centerline, when unfolded its partner should also point towards the centerline. The pentagon on the right is pointing away from the fold. When unfolded its partner should point away from the fold. Answer B is the winner. The heart shape in the middle was just extra noise as all answers have the same heart in them.

Paper Folding: Question 11

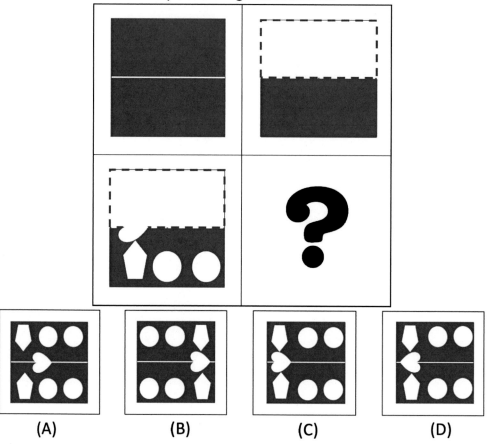

(A)   (B)   (C)   (D)

Let's do process of elimination by looking at the answers first. Each answer has a different position for the heart. Answer A is out, the heart is not above the pentagon. Answer B is out, the heart is on the wrong side. Answer D is out, the heart is pointing the wrong way. Answer C is the winner.

Paper Folding: Question 12

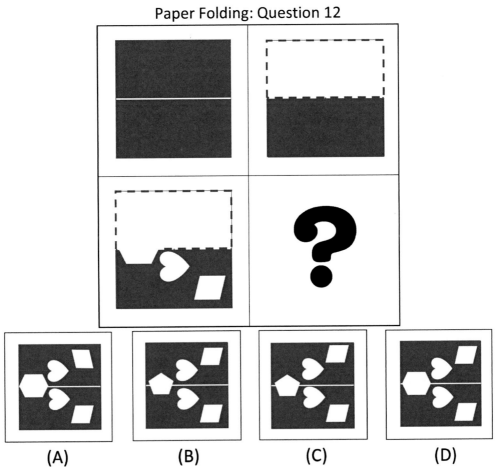

(A)   (B)   (C)   (D)

The answer is A, can you figure out why? That first shape on the left is a hexagon. Answers B and C have a pentagon which couldn't be made that way by cutting along the fold line. Compare answers A and D. The hearts are the same. The diamonds are different. Answer A's diamonds are mirror images of each other. Answer D just has the same diamond above and below the fold line. Answer A is the winner.

Paper Folding: Question 13

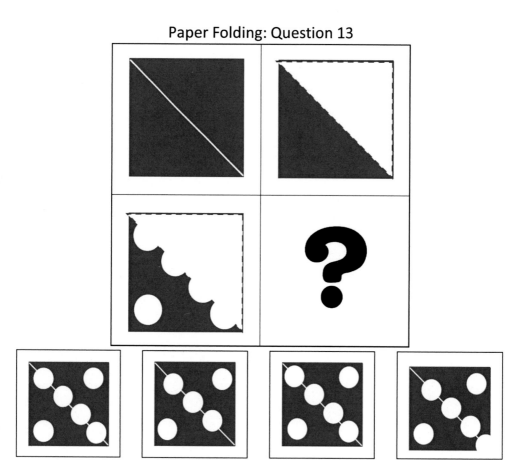

(A) (B) (C) (D)

Diagonal folds with circles should be a piece of cake by now. This one is a quick exercise in paying attention. There are four shapes cut along the centerline, so don't accidently select answer B with three shapes or answer D with the shapes in the wrong place. Answer A or C will work here.

Paper Folding: Question 14

(A) (B) (C) (D)

This question is like the last one except we add a half of a heart on the center line. That half of a heart should turn into a whole heart on the line. The circles should also stay in the corners. Is the answer A or D? The answer is D because answer A has the heart pointing in the wrong direction.

Paper Folding: Question 15

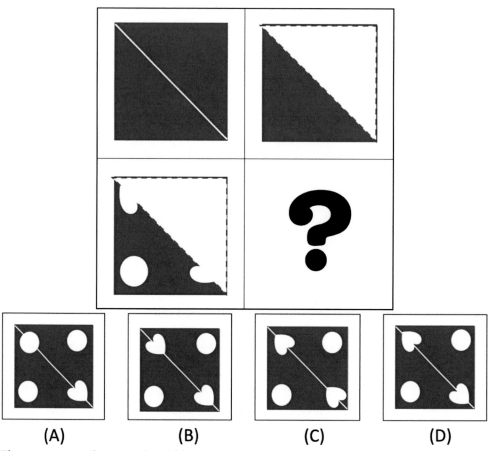

(A)   (B)   (C)   (D)

The answer to this one should have two hearts pointing away from each other and a circle in the bottom left and top right corners. Answer D is the correct answer.

Paper Folding: Question 16

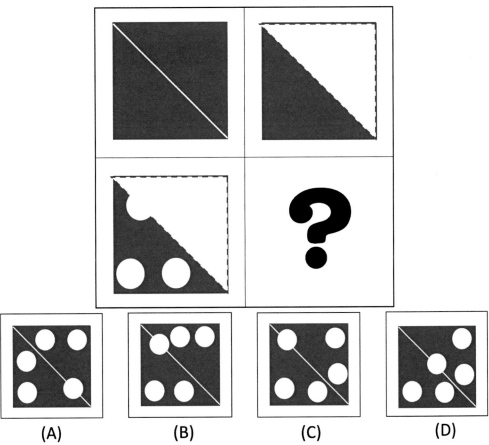

(A)   (B)   (C)   (D)

This last question is asking to pay attention to the diagonal rotation of two different dots. Take them individually instead as a whole. The bottom left dot will become a top right dot. The bottom dot will become a dot just on the other side of the fold line. The top left half circle will become a full circle along the fold line. Answer C is the winner.

Appendix D: Number Series Tips

A number series is a sequence of numbers that have a logical pattern. In this section we will train you up on some tips on how to recognize the pattern and find the best answer.

Let's start easy, can you identify the next number?

$$1 \quad 2 \quad 3 \quad 4 \quad \underline{}$$

The next number is of course 5. Why do you know that it is 5 though? You know it is 5 because you can tell that you are counting by 1, or always doing + 1.

When you do harder patterns, you can sometimes still ask yourself, "What number am I adding each time?" Try this one:

$$1 \quad 3 \quad 5 \quad 7 \quad \underline{}$$

The next number is 9. This time you were just thinking "+2" after each number.

Now try this:

$$1 \quad 1 \quad 2 \quad 3 \quad 5 \quad 8 \quad \underline{}$$

If you said the next number is 11 then you would be wrong. The correct answer is 12. In this example, we aren't adding the same number each time, so you have to remind yourself to always check the whole pattern. We are actually always adding the previous 2 numbers together to get the next number. This is a common pattern you need to recognize in math. So the pattern goes 1 + nothing is still 1, giving you your first 2 numbers 1 1. Then 1 + 1 = 2, so now your pattern is 1 1 2. Then 1 + 2 = 3 so now are pattern is 1 1 2 3. Then 2 + 3 = 5, and 3 + 5 = 8, giving us the whole pattern of 1 1 2 3 5 8. To get the next number, we add the previous 2 numbers, so we do 5 + 8 = 13, which is the correct answer.

Number series can also use subtraction:

$$10 \quad 8 \quad 6 \quad 4 \quad \underline{\quad\quad}$$

In this example what number are we always subtracting? The answer is - 2.

Number series can double:

$$1 \quad 2 \quad 4 \quad 8 \quad \underline{\quad\quad}$$

Each time the number doubles, which means it is added to itself. The next number would be 8 + 8 which means the answer is 16. If we did the next number after that it would be 16 + 16 = 32.

Sequences can divide:

40   20   10   _____

Each time the number is divided in half. To get half of a number, you have to figure out what number can be added to itself to get the answer. So are last number in this pattern is 10, what number can be added to itself to get 10? Think of it like this: ? + ? = 10? The answer is 5.

Number series can sometimes just be a pattern; there might not be any math at all:

1   12   123   _____

There is no real addition going on here. The sequence just adds the next number in the number line to it. "To get the next number add another digit on the end. This digit will be one more than the last digit in the previous number." The next number would be 1234, then 12345, then 123456 ...

Let's try some more tricks:

1   0   2   0   3   0   ____

The next number is 4. The alternating 0's are just noise to throw you off the trail. Our statement is "Add one to the last number that WASN'T a 0."

10   01   20   02   30   _____

"The next number will either be the next 10 in the series of 10's OR it will flip the tens and ones place." The last number was 30 so the next number will be 03. The next few will be 40, 04, 50, 05 ...

0001   0010   0100   _____

Binary anyone? "To get the next number move the 1 left by one place." The next number is 1000.

More Practice:

40   4   30   3   20   _____

6   6   5   5   4   _____

12   10   8   6   _____

40   35   30   25   20   _____

11   13   15   17   _____

3   6   9   12   15   _____

6   5   65 4   5   _____

7   6   7   6   7   _____

5   10 15 20 25 _____

8   6   4   2   _____

Answers:

40 4   30 3   20 2

6   6   5   5   4   4

12   10   8   6   4

40   35   30   25   20   15

11   13   15   17   19

3   6   9   12   15   18

6   5   65   4   5   45

(see we joined the 6 and the 5 to make 65? Now we join the 4 and 5 to make 45)

7   6   7   6   7   6

5   10   15   20   25   30

8   6   4   2   0

Appendix E: Number Puzzles Explained

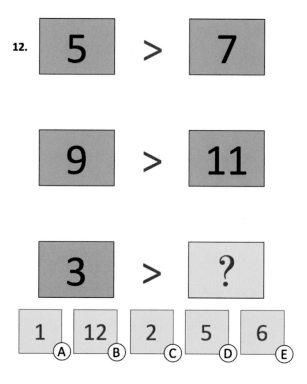

12.

5	>	7
9	>	11
3	>	?

A. 1 B. 12 C. 2 D. 5 E. 6

The number puzzles could be seen as miniature pieces of a number sequence. You are given 2 sets of numbers and you are told to figure out how they relate, then select an answer to fit the third set of numbers.

Above there are two samples:

5 turns to 7
9 turns to 11

Our logic statement "Take the number on the left and add 2 to it." Our number 3 will turn into 5. (Answer D)

The real work here is finding out how the two numbers on the left turn into the two numbers on the right and then do that same thing to the third number on the bottom.

All of the changes in number puzzles will be addition, subtraction, multiplication or division. Multiplication and division will be limited to things like doubling or halving.

Let's practice identifying how numbers change:

$$2 \rightarrow 4$$
$$4 \rightarrow 6$$

"Add 2 to the number on the left to get the number on the right" If our third number were 100 then you would look for the answer that was 100 + 2.

Try this:

$$2 \rightarrow 4$$
$$4 \rightarrow 8$$

This one looks the same but it is multiplication based. We are doubling the number. Don't be hasty! If you just looked at the first set and said "Ok 2→4, we are adding 2 to each number on the left." You'd be wrong. The lesson is to take in all of the information presented and then make your decision.

Try this:

$$10 \rightarrow 5$$
$$8 \rightarrow 4$$

"Divide the left number in half to get the right number"

And this:

15→9
20→14

"Subtract 6 from the number on the left"

More Practice:

15→20
0→5

6→12
5→10

8→4
7→3.5
6→3

21→7
6→2

0→4
7→11

7→4
15→12

Answers:

15→20
0→5
"Add 5 to the number on the left"

6→12
5→10
"Double the number on the left"

8→4
7→3.5
6→3
"Divide the number on the left in half"

21→7
6→2
"Divide the number on the left into 3 parts" or
"Divide the number on the left by 3"

0→4
7→11
"Add 4 to the number on the left"

7→4
15→12
"Subtract 3 from the number on the left"

Appendix F: Critical Thinking, Testing Tips & Exercises

Have you ever been sold on testing tips or seen testing tips as a part of the advertised education product to only see the tired list of "Be sure to eat a good breakfast!" and "Get a good night sleep!"? Well aside from quoting those worn out phrases we will not push this on you. We have actual words of wisdom to work out.

These are best served as conversation pieces or action items to be taken one or two in a setting. Each page will have its own topic of discussion, feel free to skip around.

Appendix F: Critical Thinking, Testing Tips & Exercises

What is Critical Thinking?

Critical thinking is taking information into your brain, **processing the information** and using the processed information to make better decisions.

What does that mean to "process the information"? For our purposes in the test we are mostly talking about the logic that is happening when you try to solve a problem. When looking at three shapes and trying to determine how they are similar there is a logical **loop of questions** that plays out

"Are the shapes the same color?"
"Do the shapes have the same number of sides?"
"Do the shapes point the same way?"

Processing information can also come from the student's past experience, beliefs, or other reasoning skills.

When you want to train to win the test you have to think of how you are going to process information. Then given a question type what is your loop of questions?

The next pages go into more detail on these concepts.

Appendix F: Critical Thinking, Testing Tips & Exercises

The Loop of Questions and Training Habit

A morning routine may look like this: Wake up, brush your teeth, take a shower, get dressed, eat breakfast, leave the house.

This is a cycle of actions that is taken every day and very little actual thought must be taken since it is a habit. The same idea needs to be applied to the sections of the test. You see a question and you have a list of questions to help **process the information.**

Look at these number sequences:

5	10	15	20	25
10	11	12	13	14
8	6	4	2	0

Each of these shows a different pattern but the loop of questions is the same:

"Are we adding across the sequence?"
"Are we subtracting across the sequence?"
"Are we multiplying across the sequence?"
"Are we dividing across the sequence?"

Action: On an index card develop a set of questions for each question type in this book and practice using your loop of questions. Feel free to add questions to your card as you work through the problems.

Appendix F: Critical Thinking, Testing Tips & Exercises

You Tell Me! Creating Your Own Test

Nothing helps critical thinking like having the student create their own problems. Have the student use this drawing as a template to create logic problems like the visual sections in this book.

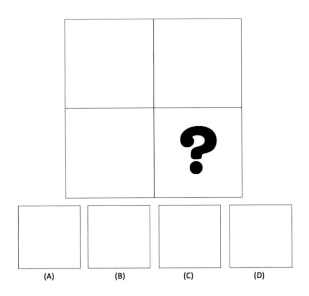

(A) (B) (C) (D)

Action: Have the student create a set of problems for you to solve on scratch paper. The questions must be logical and they must be able to explain the correct answer and why the other answers are not correct.

Bonus: Have the student create other types of questions like number strings and number puzzles.

◆ + ◆ = ? | ◆ = 3

a) 5   b) 6   c) 7   d) 8   e) 9

Appendix F: Critical Thinking, Testing Tips & Exercises

Question Each Answer

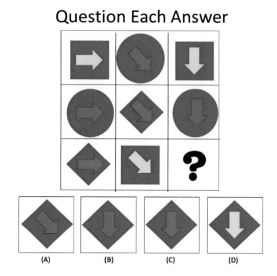

The test is asking you questions. Turn the tables and ask questions of the test! Here we want to find the right picture to fit the bottom right block. Let's have an imaginary conversation

You: "Answer A-D Why are you not the correct answer?"
Answer A: "I'm a blue diamond with a green arrow pointing diagonally. I am in the third column where all arrows point down. I am probably not the answer"
Answer B: "I have a green arrow that points down. I am pointing the right way but each row has the third arrow the same color as the first arrow. I should be red"
Answer C: "I am a red arrow pointing down, I may be the right answer"
Answer D: "I am a yellow arrow pointing down, I am not the right answer"

Action: Try questioning answers with a few practice problems in each section.

Test Each Answer

Similar to question each answer, we will now test each answer. This is a very powerful tool in acing any type of multiple choice algebra type test.

Look at this number series

$$4 \quad 5 \quad 45 \quad 6 \quad 7 \quad \underline{\quad\quad}$$

A) 7   B)8   C)21   D) 4   E)67

This looks like a simple addition, add each number to the last. But what is that 45 in the middle of the string for? Well test each answer and see if it looks like it can fit mentally place each answer into the space and see if it looks right. Answer E is correct. Once placed in the answer spot you may "see the pattern" 4 and 5 become 45; 6 and 7 become 67!

Look at this Number Puzzle

| | a) 7 | b) 6 | c) 5 | d) 8 | e) 9 |

Substitute the Triangle for the 4 and require the problem as 4 + 3 on your scratch paper. Now we have 4 + 3 = ? Replace the answers presented to see which one fits the problem. 4 + 3 = 7? Yes, the answer is A.

Appendix F: Critical Thinking, Testing Tips & Exercises

Mental Gymnastics for Attention to Detail

In grade school you are given a sheet of math, it may have 5 or 10 of the same type of problem. Maybe you get 10 addition and 10 subtraction problems. You do the 10 addition problems, then do the 10 subtraction problems. Your ability to pay attention to detail is slightly dropped as you work through 10 of the same type of problem. You don't have to think "Oh this is an addition problem...what are the rules for addition?...ok time to do addition" You know all 10 are addition so you work them like an assembly line.

Action: Instead of working 10 of the same type of problem work one problem from each of the 9 sets in this book. The process of switching problem types after each problem forces you to examine the rule set.

"Ok it's a number series, in these the series could be addition, subtraction, multiplication or division"

"Ok it's picture categories I need to look for similar shapes, counts, colors, sides and so on."

Appendix F: Critical Thinking, Testing Tips & Exercises

Proverbs for Exercising Analysis Skills

Define Analysis: examination of something. Breaking complicated things into smaller parts to gain understanding.

Analysis is determining the intended meaning of some bit of information. When you analyze pictures for categories you are breaking the pictures into smaller parts to understand them. "Does each picture have a triangle?" is a good analysis question.

Here we will recognize your analysis skills by discussing proverbs. A proverb is a simple saying that has a deeper meaning. First break the proverb into parts, try to understand the parts and then guess at the overall meaning.

Have the student tell you what each of these proverbs means after their careful analysis.

"The early bird gets the worm"

"There is more to knowing than just being correct"

"A book holds a house of gold"

"A diamond with a flaw is worth more than a perfect pebble"

"Deep doubts, doubts, deep wisdom; small doubts, little wisdom"

"Dig the water well before you are thirsty"

This concludes our book. Be sure to check out our COGAT® Trainer apps on iTunes and Google Play. Just search for Kindergarten COGAT® and look for Polemics Applications.

Send all feedback good to polemicsapp@yahoo.com